MICHAEL VICK

FINALLY FREE AN AUTOBIOGRAPHY

MICHAEL VICK

FINALLY FREE AN AUTOBIOGRAPHY

by
Michael Vick with
Brett Honeycutt and
Stephen Copeland

Published by Worthy Publishing, a division of Worthy Media, Inc., 134 Franklin Road, Suite 200, Brentwood, Tennessee 37027.

Published in association with The Core Media Group, Inc., P.O. Box 2037, Indian Trail, North Carolina 28079.

HELPING PEOPLE EXPERIENCE THE HEART OF GOD

eBook available at www.worthypublishing.com

Audio distributed through Oasis Audio; visit www.oasisaudio.com

Library of Congress Control Number: 2011935243

Unless otherwise indicated, Scripture quotations in this book are taken from The Holy Bible, *New International Version*®, *NIV*®. Copyright © 1973, 1978, 1984, 2011 by Biblica, Inc.™ Used by permission. All rights reserved worldwide.

Scripture quotations marked (KJV) are taken from the King James Version of the Bible.

For foreign and subsidiary rights, contact Riggins International Rights Services, Inc.; www.rigginsrights.com

ISBN: 978-1-617950-69-8 (hardcover w/ jacket)

Cover and Interior Design: Renata Bolden
Cover Photo: Jeff Livengood
Additional Images: Greg Arnold and Aaron May

Printed in the United States of America
12 13 14 15 16 17 LBM 8 7 6 5 4 3 2 1

For my grandmother, Caletha Vick, who passed away on May 2, 2008.

When I was a young boy, she instilled in me wisdom and understanding. She was the rock in my life and taught me what the truly important things are.

It hurt me that I didn't have the chance to spend time with her and talk with her before I got out of prison. It was my hope to be out before she died, but that didn't happen.

She will always be a part of me, because with her is where the dream began. It was her encouragement, love, and support that pushed me to dream.

She's the reason I'm living my dream.

I could never thank her enough. I will always love and miss her deeply.

CONTENTS

Foreword

The first time I saw Michael Vick play football was in January of 2000 in the Sugar Bowl. He was a freshman quarterback at Virginia Tech and his team was playing Florida State for the national championship. I was the head coach of the Tampa Bay Buccaneers at the time. Our Bucs teams were known for their defense (in fact, we would play in the NFC Championship game later that month and hold one of the greatest offenses of all time, the 1999 St. Louis Rams, to eleven points).

I had seen Florida State's defenses quite a bit over the years. We had drafted four defenders from Florida State in the previous five years, including future Hall of Famer Derrick Brooks. But that year Florida State had what I considered the best, and fastest, college defense I had ever seen.

However, Michael Vick put on a show that night in the Sugar Bowl and vaulted into the national spotlight. He was unquestionably the best player on the field. Florida State's vaunted defense could not contain him as he threw, ran, and led his team back from a 21-point deficit to take the lead. Virginia Tech would eventually lose that game 46-29, but Michael had concluded the most dominant year any freshman quarterback had ever had.

That performance, more than anything else, convinced the Atlanta Falcons to select Michael with the first pick in the 2001 NFL draft. Once with the Falcons, Michael continued to electrify fans with highlight-reel plays and, in his second year, led them to the brink of a Super Bowl. By that time, I was head coach of the Indianapolis Colts and in my twenty-third year of coaching in the NFL. I had never seen a weapon like Vick at the quarterback position. He had one of the strongest arms to ever play the game, and on most days he was the fastest player on the field. His potential seemed unlimited; he had become an icon to the young sports fans of the new millennium—a flashy superhero to the so-called Generation X.

By the end of the 2004 season, Michael seemed to have the world at his feet. He was young, talented, and one of the most popular players in the most popular sport in America. But there were things going on in Michael's private life that sports fans didn't know about. At the height of his popularity, Michael's career was about to come to a screeching halt.

Michael and I first met in August of 2005 in Tokyo, Japan. The Colts were playing the Falcons, and we did some joint press conferences to promote the game. It allowed me the opportunity to tell him how much I enjoyed watching him play. Spending some time with him, I discovered he loved fishing as much as I did, and we talked about getting an outing together back in the US. We tried, but were never successful in setting up a date that worked for both of us.

That has been one of my biggest regrets, because the next time we actually talked face-to-face was June of 2009, in the visitors' quarters at Leavenworth Federal Penitentiary in Kansas, after Mike had been convicted on charges of running a dogfighting operation.

We spent about three hours talking at the prison that day, and we covered a lot of subjects. We talked a little about playing football and about the NFL. We talked about growing up, families, friends, and children. We talked about decision making, role modeling, and responsibility. But, more than anything else, we talked about the Lord—about what role God had played in Michael's life, and what God might have in store for him in the future.

Michael shared with me how he had drifted away from the Christian faith in which his grandmother had raised him. I gave him a little advice that my dad had passed on to me years ago: "When you have a problem, don't dwell on where you are but spend your energy thinking about how you're going to make the situation better."

That day I asked Michael what he wanted to do moving forward. He said he wanted to make sure his children grew up with their dad around, leading them in the right direction. He wanted the young people who had cheered for him to know that, although he had made some mistakes, he wasn't a bad person. And thirdly, he wanted to come back to the NFL and be a better quarterback than he was when he left.

We agreed it wouldn't be easy, given the public opinion that was so against him at the time. I had gotten letters and phone calls vilifying me for even going to see him, so I couldn't imagine what he would face once he got out. He was going to have to do it with actions, not words. With God's help, I believed he could do the first two, but even I didn't have faith he could accomplish the last. Michael promised me he would achieve all three.

Since that day we have stayed in touch. We call and text each other quite regularly, and Michael has kept his promise to me. He has been there for his family, and I know he's going to be the husband and father that they need. He's been active in the community—especially with young people, encouraging them to make good life choices and urging them to think about their futures. And yes, with the help of Philadelphia head coach Andy Reid and the Philadelphia Eagles, he has become a better quarterback than ever. In the fan voting for the 2011 Pro Bowl, Michael was the second-leading vote-getter, just behind Tom Brady and topping Peyton Manning—something I would have thought impossible that day at Leavenworth.

Finally Free tells an amazing story. It's not all pretty, but it's real. If you're like me—if you've ever done something in your life you wish you could take back—it will encourage you to learn that we serve a God of second chances and live in a country of second chances.

The story is not complete, by any means, but this book will let you know why I'm so proud of Michael Vick and honored to call him a friend—because he has made the later chapters of his life better than the earlier ones.

And isn't that what life is all about?

—Tony Dungy

Acknowledgments

I would like to give a special thanks to Tony Dungy, Roger Goodell, Jeffrey Lurie, and Andy Reid for believing in me and giving me a second chance.

Also, I want to thank my agent, Joel Segal; my publicist, Chris Shigas; and Rick French, for all of their hard work and for helping me get my career back on track.

There are so many people who have had a great impact on my life. To Pastor Kelley, thank you for your prayers and discipleship. To Coach Reamon, thank you for teaching me. To Coach Beamer, thank you for leading me. To Mr. Blank, thank you for first giving me an opportunity and then for your forgiveness. To Danny, thank you for all of your hard work, guidance, and counsel. And to Woody, thank you for your continued support and for always having my back.

Brett and Steve, I can't thank you enough for assisting me in putting my story and feelings on paper. And thanks to The Core Media Group for giving me the opportunity to share my story and provide hope and inspiration for others.

But most importantly I would like to thank my family, friends, everyone who visited me in Kansas, and my current and former teammates for being there for me at a time in my life when I needed them most. Thank you.

Lastly, I want to acknowledge the love and grace of God; without Him, I would not have a story to share.

Introduction

When the idea for this book was first conceived, Michael Vick was a backup quarterback. He wanted to tell his story so that other people, particularly youth, could learn from his mistakes.

He wanted to express yet again his sincere apologies for getting involved in a barbaric dogfighting operation that landed him in jail for eighteen months, plus two months of home confinement and three years of probation after that.

He wanted to share some of what life was like behind bars and how his relationship with God was rekindled during those dreary days of incarceration.

He wanted to talk about the absolute joy of getting a second chance to play in the National Football League, even if he was mostly watching from the sidelines.

There was no indication then that Vick, a former three-time Pro Bowler with the Atlanta Falcons, would do anything other than run a few plays out of the Wildcat formation for the Philadelphia Eagles during the 2010 season, just as he had done in '09.

But then there was a telephone conversation—Vick with his former high school coach, Tommy Reamon, on the eve of the Eagles' season-opening game against the Green Bay Packers.

Reamon says he told Vick the game would change his life. Vick didn't quite know what to make of such a bold statement.

But Reamon was right. Eagles' starter Kevin Kolb was injured in the first half, and Vick entered the game and played extremely well in the second half. From that point on—even when he was out with a rib injury for three games—Vick became firmly established as the Eagles' starting quarterback.

He played with a maturity and a precision in the passing game that he'd never displayed in Atlanta. Yet he still possessed those magic legs with the nifty moves that had made him such a threat to run with the Falcons.

As the 2010 season went along, Vick's resurgence quickly became the story of the season in the NFL. He appeared on the cover of *Sports Illustrated*. He was interviewed at length by virtually every major sports television network.

He was back—all the way back, better than ever.

He turned in a performance for the ages against the Washington Redskins on *Monday Night Football*, accounting for six touchdowns—four passing and two running. He led the league in passing for weeks and eventually became the leading NFC vote-getter in fan balloting for the Pro Bowl and the second-leading vote-getter in the NFL.

Imagine that: just a few months earlier, the same person who was voted the most disliked athlete in America was now receiving more Pro Bowl votes from fans than nearly any other player. Obviously forgiveness, redemption, and second chances remain cornerstones of our society.

The man who suspended him from the NFL, league commissioner Roger Goodell, was quoted late in the season as saying he was proud of Vick and cited as exemplary the way Vick was trying to be a model for others on and off the field, which included regularly giving talks denouncing dogfighting on behalf of the Humane Society of the United States.

Then, in early December, the same US District Court judge who had sentenced Vick to prison, the Honorable Henry E. Hudson, praised Vick's progress in an interview with the *Washington Post*. "He's an example of how the system can work," said Hudson. "He's having a terrific season. I'm very happy for him. I wish him the best of success."

What Goodell and Judge Hudson did, in effect, was put the matter back in our hands. We were each left to determine what we were going to do with the Vick issue. Would we forgive?

This, then, is a story as much about the rest of us as it is about Michael Vick. It will chronicle perhaps the most remarkable personal and professional turnaround in pro sports history.

Part I:

The Rise

Chapter One

In the Beginning

"The beginning of my love for football goes back to when I was seven years old."

Hokies.

　　Falcons.

　　Eagles.

I've always been a bird.

I went from the ground—a foundation of faith and family that positioned me for success . . . to the air—a dangerous and selfish rise that took me higher and higher in flight . . . to a crash—a wounding yet deserved fall that took me lower and lower . . . to the cage—a humbling and desolate state that helped me return to the ground, rediscover my foundation, long for redemption, and ignite a strong desire to change.

To change and rise again . . .

⌒

After everything I have been through in my life and football career, it was surreal to be back in Hawaii for the Pro Bowl in January 2011.

I sat in the middle of the bus that was transporting the NFC team from our hotel to the practice field, surrounded by three star players from my former team, the Atlanta Falcons. Wide receiver Roddy White was to my back right, quarterback Matt Ryan was directly across the aisle from me, and running back Michael Turner sat directly in front of me. We talked some, but mostly Matt and Roddy kidded Michael Turner about his eating.

It was so ironic that we were sitting together. I spent six years with the Falcons, making the Pro Bowl on three occasions, and even though my time with them didn't end anything like I or anyone else expected, I still have a fondness in my heart for that organization. I forever will.

Once the bus arrived, I was amazed at the scene that was in front of me. Fans packed the path to the practice field. I saw reporters, cameras, and banners welcoming everyone to the 2011 Pro Bowl—the all-star game that follows each NFL season. It's one of the greatest honors in the league to be selected for the game, especially since your peers and fans both get to vote.

The sun was shining bright that day. It was beautiful. Everyone I looked at had a smile on his or her face, especially the children. They wanted to get helmets and other items signed. I tried to sign as many autographs as possible, but the security officers assigned to us kept ushering me toward the field.

It was a long but incredible walk. I felt such a sense of accomplishment as I looked at all the great players around me. I felt a sense of belonging. It was so rewarding to feel like I was back on the right track.

I kept having flashbacks, though.

I thought about my two long years away from football, when I didn't know if I would ever make it back to the Pro Bowl.

I thought about how hard I worked to get there again and the incredible opportunity the Philadelphia Eagles gave me with a second chance to play in the NFL.

And I thought about my childhood years, when I first dreamed of playing in the NFL. Back then, in the beginning, being in a place like Hawaii was beyond my wildest imagination.

I grew up in the Ridley Circle housing project—unit 667—in the crime-infested East End of Newport News, Virginia. Back then, I was known as "Ookie," a nickname that was given to me by my Aunt Tina shortly after I was born, on June 26, 1980.

The environment I grew up in played a tremendous part in my youth. There were consequences—both good and bad—that I had to deal with.

Newport News is sometimes referred to as "NewportNam"—a word twist on "Vietnam." The inference is that Newport News is a jungle-like war zone with pitfalls and traps at every turn. You just never knew when a peaceful situation would turn into a violent, volatile situation.

In and around where I lived, anyone could get shot at any time or place. Anyone could be the main target. And anyone could be in the wrong place at the wrong time and caught in the line of fire. It was rough for the people who lived there.

One summer growing up, I heard a gunshot every night. I vividly remember being awakened one night by a sharp *POP*. I jumped up. The shot was so loud and clear because we had to sleep with the windows open; it was really hot, and we didn't have central air upstairs.

You reach a point where you become immune to the violence and crime; the sounds of gunfire became white noise that faded into the background of our lives. It was common to see guys walking through the neighborhood with shotguns and rifles. They were either headed to an altercation, or would start one because they were carrying guns and acting "tough." You'd see fights all the time—fistfights, and even domestic family fights. It was crazy in that area—a living environment many people can't comprehend.

You had to watch your back and be cautious of where you were. So many people—good people—fell victim because they weren't aware of their surroundings.

One of those victims was a close friend of mine, Abdullah McClane, who was known to the rest of us simply as "Peahead." As just a young teen, he was shot walking near the Food Tiger store on Hampton Avenue.

I was crushed when I heard about it. Before, I had been immune to the gunfire, but now it had real consequences. My world changed that day. I lost my friend.

We had been teammates in Pop Warner football, and the plan was for us to play together all the way up through high school. Peahead was going to be the quarterback, and I was going to be the running back. He was good—better than me, actually. And, coincidentally, he was a left-hander too, just like me.

But those were my surroundings. Anything could happen to anyone at any time. It's what we all dealt with on a daily basis and why I wanted to escape from Ridley Circle.

My escape came through football.

⌐⌐

Ironically, my roots in football come from the Washington Redskins—the same Washington Redskins that I would play my career game against in 2010, cementing my return to professional football. Sometimes it's the moments that take us back to the beginning that are most important.

The beginning of my love for football goes back to when I was seven years old. I was spending time with my grandmother, Caletha Vick. I never knew anything about the game until one Sunday afternoon when she turned on the television because the Redskins were playing. They were my Uncle Casey's favorite team—and my grandmother's favorite too.

After watching the game with them, I was hooked; my fascination grew deep inside me. At that moment, I knew playing in the NFL was what I wanted to do when I grew up.

"I'm going to play professional football someday," I told her.

"Well, you have to learn how to play then," I remember her saying. "Ask your uncle because he played in high school."

From that day on, I carried a football with me everywhere I

went in the neighborhood. As time went by, I played more and more, getting better every day.

I was highly competitive, a trait that was developed not only in Pop Warner but also in impromptu games and scrimmages that broke out on the street before school began.

We used to play tackle against other neighborhoods—against guys who were bigger and stronger than us. We were little guys, but hey, we wanted the older guys in our neighborhood to view us as good football players, and we wanted to be the best. So by playing against the bigger kids, we had to work harder and be faster. It was great practice.

We played tag football in the street in the mornings before our school bus arrived and were usually sweating when we climbed on the bus. It was how everyone honed their skills. It was why we were so much better than the other youth league football teams we played. We were practicing all the time.

My first position for the Boys & Girls Club Spartans was tight end, which I didn't like. I was a good receiver, but the problem was that I also had to block, and I didn't like contact. I didn't even know what I was doing. The whole time I played in games that year, I was looking at my mom on the sideline and was really ready to go home. The next season, however, I was moved to quarterback, and on my very first pass I threw a touchdown.

I didn't even see what happened because I was so short. I dropped back and threw the ball as far as I could to my receiver, Corey Barnes. The next thing I knew, the coaches started jumping up and down, and people started grabbing me. I was so happy and excited. I loved that feeling. I chased that feeling.

$$\sim$$

One thing I can certainly say about my youth is that it wasn't difficult to find trouble in the streets.

I wasn't a troublemaker per se, but I hung around with guys who caused a good deal of trouble. They were constantly getting into fights, stealing bikes, and taking stuff from people's yards and local stores. My childhood best friend, Jamel Wilson, and I were never into all that. We showed respect to the other guys and the older kids in the neighborhood, and they had respect for us because we didn't get involved in the neighborhood nonsense. For me it was more fun to play football than to fight or steal.

But I wasn't an angel by any means either; I had my moments of childhood indiscretion and mischief. I snuck down to a place called The Crab Factory and stole seafood to sell elsewhere in the neighborhood. I also would ride my bike or even walk miles farther away from our house than my parents knew.

The thing is, I had four great influences keeping me from getting into too much trouble: my mother, Brenda Vick; my grandmother; the outlet of sports; and especially the Boys & Girls Club, which was located a short walk from home.

My mom was, and is, the rock of our family. I have a younger brother, Marcus, and two sisters: Christina, who is the oldest, and Courtney, the baby of the family. Mom took on all the responsibilities of raising us. Even though my dad, Michael Boddie, was there, Mom dedicated herself to making sure that we were provided for and that we lived the best life we could.

She was a very forgiving lady—very generous and gracious. But she was stern and didn't hesitate to correct us by chastising or spanking us. And when need be, the belt came out. But we needed it. God knows I did!

For some reason, when I was away from the house, I was a cool, calm guy. But when I was home with my mom, I would just wreak havoc all over the house. My mom would put the belt to me when she needed to. Of course, I didn't want to be punished, but it did keep me in line.

She always made sure we had the finer things in life to the extent we could afford them. If it was one new pair of shoes per year, she was going to make sure they were clean, and she was going to make sure we had brand-new clothes to wear with them. Mom just dedicated herself to giving us the best life possible. She worked two jobs at times and did everything she could to provide. It's amazing what she did for us on the income she earned from working at Super Kmart.

She found a way to keep us away from potential harm too. She tried to show us a different side of life when she could. For instance, she took us to Outback Steakhouse whenever she had enough money so we could eat somewhere nice. She sacrificed a lot for us.

My father worked in the nearby shipyards as a sandblaster, turning in long hours that kept him away from the family. But it wasn't just his job that kept him away and distant at times. He also spent plenty of time in the streets, struggling with drugs and alcohol.

He would stay with us at our house, but he really wouldn't put in the effort and family time like I thought he should have. I guess he was into his own thing. I can't really put my finger on it, but I wanted something more. I wanted to spend time with my dad, but he wasn't there. He was usually running with his friends. But he showed that he cared by making sure things were okay for us financially.

I do have some great memories with my dad. When we did spend time together, he would take the time to throw the football with me in the yard. It was in those early days that I realized I was a left-handed passer, which makes me somewhat unique in a sport in which right-handed quarterbacks are most prevalent.

My mother and father eventually married. To my best friend, Jamel, our family seemed close-knit since there was a father and mother in the home. He said we were just about the only family in the neighborhood with a mother and a father in the home together. Jamel once told me, "You have the complete family. You have what everybody else wants." He also said he fondly remembers my mother bringing out cookies, candy, and chips for all the kids in the neighborhood to enjoy.

Jamel's perception wasn't far off. Although my father struggled and may have been separated or distant from us at times, the rest of our family was tight. My brother, sisters, and I joked and played pranks on one another. For some reason, I specifically remember my brother flipping the light switch and acting like he was being electrocuted. My sister would go bananas.

Besides being practical jokers, we also played different games and had fun contests around the house. Thursday nights were pizza night. We would stay home, order pizza, sit cross-legged, and everyone would have a good time and laugh and joke. We were competitive in everything. We stayed up and played cards late at night, talking and enjoying time with each other. We played spades, war, checkers, and one of my favorite games, Monopoly. In Monopoly, I won all the time. I always had the most money and properties.

Back then, money seemed easier to manage.

I was especially close to my grandmother and spent many memorable times with her. Every weekend, my sisters and I would stay over at her house. I laugh now, remembering how I would flee to her for refuge.

When my mom was mad at me, or whenever I got in trouble and got a spanking, I would usually go to my grandmother's house. She was my getaway. She was my hideout. And she spoiled me to death.

If the trash was full, I would take it out, and she would give me a quarter. When I came in at the right time, she would also give me a quarter, enough for me to go get some candy from the store. She was an incredibly loving lady who always cared about us. If anything was wrong with our health, she felt like she could cure us. If I went to her house on the way to school and said I was tired, she would let me stay home, and I wouldn't have to go to school. If only my mother knew . . .

Always a positive influence (even when I stayed home from school), she instilled in me that I had to have the inner strength to overcome adversity. I can remember her saying, "You make sure you take advantage of every opportunity you can in life and make sure you take your education seriously, because nothing is going to be easy." At that time, when I was young, I didn't understand what she was saying, but she was right. Taking advantage of every opportunity is something I wish I had done.

My grandmother also introduced me to the Christian faith. She took me to Solid Rock Church, located in our neighborhood close to where we lived. Those times established an important foundation that I later turned to in my most trying moments.

During my sophomore year of high school, I started sleeping with the Bible under my pillow. I felt like it protected me, and I wanted to be closer to God. As I read the Bible at a young age, I tried to get a clearer understanding of what was written. But I really needed some counsel, discipleship, and education about what I was reading. Even though I wasn't able to grasp everything on my own, I was able to build that sense of belief, knowing that I could do all things through God and that I couldn't do it without Him.

My favorite Scripture passage growing up was Psalm 23, which, in the King James Version of the Bible, says:

The LORD is my shepherd; I shall not want.

He maketh me to lie down in green pastures:

he leadeth me beside the still waters.

He restoreth my soul: he leadeth me in the paths of

righteousness for his name's sake.

Yea, though I walk through the valley of the shadow of

death, I will fear no evil: for thou art with me;

thy rod and thy staff they comfort me.

Thou preparest a table before me in the presence of

mine enemies: thou anointest my head with oil;

my cup runneth over.

Surely goodness and mercy shall follow me all the days

of my life: and I will dwell in the house of

the LORD for ever.

My favorite verse of Scripture, Jeremiah 29:11, is one that my grandmother always told me to read:

"For I know the plans I have for you," declares the LORD,

"plans to prosper you and not to harm you, plans to

give you hope and a future."

I know the other kids in the neighborhood weren't sleeping with the Bible under their pillows; they weren't reading their Bible at night. None of my friends were doing it. I was probably the only kid in Newport News who was. The reason I say that is to highlight my solid foundation. Though gunshots echoed through the night in Newport News, my personal foundation—thanks to my mother and grandmother—was rock solid.

I practiced this discipline from when I was about fifteen until shortly before I was drafted into the NFL. For me, in connection with my grandmother's support, reading the Bible provided me a solid center and balance for my life. It kept me focused. Turning away from that practice and no longer sleeping with it under my pillow was symbolic of my turning away from God and leaning on my own understanding, which was a huge mistake.

Later in life, when I went to prison, the Bible returned to its rightful place—under my pillow. But it never should have left.

I don't know what would have happened to me during my youth if I had not had the local Boys & Girls Club as a place to spend my time productively, participating in sports and other group activities. It was a sanctuary for me. It may have saved my life.

The man who was in charge of the club, Mr. James "Poo" Johnson, was a key mentor early in my life. He was an outstanding man for any kid to have in their journey through life. He kept everything on even ground and even keel. He was there for us. He was very inspirational and encouraged us to do our best. He wanted us to, and hoped we would, come to the Boys & Girls Club each and every day.

Realizing that many of us didn't have father figures in our lives, he felt a sense of responsibility to take on that role. He was a loving guy, but he was also a disciplinarian in a sense. He was stern and didn't allow us to do whatever we wanted.

One thing I remember about Mr. Johnson was that he had a box of yock—a type of beef noodle soup—from the 18th Street Chinese food store every Friday. When I was a kid, a box of yock was seven bucks. My mother could only get it on Fridays too—when she and my dad got paid. When Mr. Johnson had his, I wanted to ask him for some, but I couldn't muster the courage because I thought it'd be disrespectful. But I wanted it *so* bad. To this day, every time I see a box of yock, I think of Mr. Johnson.

Mr. Johnson remembers me as being not only highly athletic at a young age but also very competitive. He says that he remembers sitting me down a couple times and telling me, "You can't win everything."

His goal then was the same as it is today—for the Newport News Boys & Girls Club to be a safe haven for children from the negative influences all around them. He understood that, because of where I was living, I had a lot of distractions that could've been disastrous for me if it wasn't for the Boys & Girls Club.

Mr. Johnson had high expectations for me and tried to be a "tell it like it is" mentor. He gave it to me straight—whether I liked hearing it or not. I'm glad Mr. Johnson did. I needed it that way.

After my prison sentence, I returned to the Boys & Girls Club to work for Mr. Johnson.

I went back to my roots—back to the start.

⌒

Another very important mentor over the years was Coach Tommy Reamon, a former professional running back who became a high school coach in the Newport News area. When I was in the eighth grade, he saw early glimpses of raw talent that needed to be developed and thought that I could become a special player.

Even then, I possessed a desire to escape the projects by playing pro football someday. I asked him if he could help me get a college scholarship like my cousin—quarterback Aaron Brooks—who played at the University of Virginia and later in the NFL with the New Orleans Saints and Oakland Raiders from 2000 to 2007. And Coach Reamon willingly and sacrificially helped me.

Like me, Coach Reamon grew up in the rough East End of Newport News, and he knew what it took to escape. He played college football at Missouri before being drafted in 1974 by the Pittsburgh Steelers of the NFL and the Florida Blazers of the World Football League, where he had an MVP year his rookie season. He later told me, "You had to dream to get out of that neighborhood."

Coach Reamon provided a tremendous amount of support and guidance for me. He believed in me so much that, when I was a sophomore, he took me to the University of Virginia football camp, paying out of his own pocket. He was trying to help me become the best quarterback I could be, and that experience— being around the best players in Virginia—helped catapult me to a different level.

I had only known him for a year at that point, and he had a son of his own, but he *chose* to make personal sacrifices for *me*. He didn't have to drive me two hours to UVA. He didn't have to help me become a better player. But he did. It was scary, because those four days at UVA were my first time away from my family. But at the same time, I wasn't away from family. That's because Coach Reamon became a dependable father figure for me that weekend. I had family with me.

When I made it to the NFL—something that would not have happened without Coach Reamon's help—I began to neglect our relationship and focus on myself. He called me his "son." He treated me like a son. And I recklessly abandoned our relationship because I was becoming a "me" guy.

Not talking to him once I made it to the NFL was one of the worst things I could have done. It's probably one of the reasons things ended up the way they did. Upon my release from prison, we rekindled our father-and-son relationship.

Again, I went back to my roots—back to the start.

Chapter Two

Seven's Heaven

"It fit me."

My No. 7 Philadelphia Eagles jersey became one of the NFL's best-selling jerseys again in 2010 after topping the charts at times during my stay in Atlanta. I guess you could say the number is as much a fixture on me as No. 18 is on Peyton Manning and No. 12 is on Tom Brady.

I like the fact that the number has biblical significance. Someone told me that it's considered God's "perfect" number by many theologians. For instance, there are seven days in a week, making the number symbolic of completion.

I didn't start out with 7 as my number during my high school days, however. I wore No. 11 playing for Coach Reamon during my freshman and sophomore seasons at Ferguson High in Newport News and initially was given No. 1 when I transferred to Warwick High with Coach Reamon when Ferguson closed down in 1996.

At first I liked my new number. My archrival was quarterback Ronald Curry at nearby Hampton High. Ronald received more fanfare than I did back in those days, so when Coach Reamon gave me No. 1, I saw it as a vote of confidence that he considered me the best quarterback around.

It was nice, but something about the number didn't seem to fit me (yes, I admit to being just a bit superstitious). The entire time I wore No. 1, things just didn't go right for me. I couldn't complete any passes, and I remember having a really, really bad scrimmage.

The next week in practice—and I'm the team leader, remember—I was lying on the ground thinking, *How can I get better? How can I gain the confidence of my teammates entering my junior year?* I looked over at my friend Andrae Harrison, who was our top receiver at the time, and said, "Andrae, let's exchange jerseys. Let's switch numbers."

He said, "Are you serious? I thought you wanted to wear No. 1."

I told him, "Yeah, I just need a change."

So we switched, and I put on the No. 7 jersey that Andrae was wearing. I've kept it ever since.

My career took off from that exact point. I had a great practice that day, and I felt like a totally different person. The number actually looked good on me! It fit me. Everyone told me, "I like you a lot better in No. 7 than in No. 1."

Coach Reamon just laughs at the memory.

~~

One thing No. 7 could not do was make me the No. 1 high school quarterback in Newport News. That belonged to Hampton's Ronald Curry. All through high school, I lived in his shadow. The newspapers routinely had a huge picture of Ronald, and at the bottom, a tiny picture of me about the size of a stamp.

My whole high school career can be described as me trying to emulate someone who, I believe, is the best to ever play high school football. After every game, I read his stats in the newspaper. I looked at his picture—saw his socks, his uniform, what kind of shoes he was wearing. Anytime I had the opportunity to watch Ronald play, I went to Hampton's games. I dissected his style of football—his leadership, his moves, his stats. Everything he did was engrained in my memory bank. He probably didn't do the same with me—he was No. 1.

Living in Ronald's shadow ended up being great for my career. He made me a better player. Made me dream bigger. Made me play harder. Made me want to improve. Made me want to be the best. The best ever.

In football, you need people to push you. You need a backup quarterback to push you. You need coaches to push you. Ronald was my push. I saw his stats and knew they were better. I saw his team's record and knew they were better. But I could not say to myself that he was better than me. I was always struggling with that internally, but I never let it out. I didn't want anyone to catch the vibe that there was any form of hatred, jealousy, or envy toward Ronald. Though I *was* jealous, I admired him too much to let that out.

Now, don't get me wrong. Though Ronald Curry was Virginia's main attraction, I still stood out—especially to Coach Reamon.

Even back in my days at Ferguson—in my first two high school seasons—Coach Reamon saw something special in me. He marveled at my arm strength and a throwing motion that featured a flick of the wrist.

"It's unique," Coach Reamon told me. "There are very few players who do that." But we both knew that it worked.

I spent most of my freshman season at Ferguson with the junior varsity but was elevated to varsity for the final three games of the season. I remember throwing for over 430 yards with four touchdowns in my second varsity start, a 41-14 win over Gloucester.

After transferring to Warwick for my last two high school seasons, my skills improved and I became more successful. My favorite play came in a game against Denbigh High. I remember it vividly. I scrambled to my right and I had three guys coming at me. I made a move that was so "freaky" that Coach Reamon was like, "Son, when I saw you make that move right there, I knew you were going to play in the NFL."

He said he had never, in his history of watching football, seen anyone make a move as quick and as agile as I did. The truth is, it was actually a bad play—an incomplete pass—but the way I improvised, I guess, just made people see that I had potential.

Coach Reamon began to utilize my speed at other positions too. In 1997 at Warwick, I bookended my senior season with a pair of punt returns for touchdowns. In our first game of the season against Phoebus, I returned a punt 70-some yards for a touchdown, and in my high school finale against Woodside, I had a 35-yard punt return for a touchdown.

My running ability became more noticeable in my junior year and really blossomed my senior season. Hundred-yard rushing games became more common. I noticed I was faster than other players. The game slowed down for me. Teams changed their defenses just for me. People said I was "elusive." They said I was a "new kind of quarterback."

Even though I accomplished a great deal, one of the disappointing aspects of my high school career is that I never played in the Virginia state playoffs. I don't dwell on it, though. I knew we didn't have the same talent or size that some other teams did, and I couldn't change that. However, I'm glad that I never played on a team with a losing record in high school. We were 5-5 twice at Ferguson, and we were 6-4 and 7-3 at Warwick. But I wanted to be better. I wanted to win. I wanted to be No. 1.

During our senior season, I had the chance to play my rival, Ronald Curry. The game drew a lot of attention. Eight thousand people came to see us play. It was an opportunity to emerge from Ronald's shadow.

Before the game, Coach Reamon talked to me. "Virginia Tech called and wants to offer you a scholarship," he said. "But it'll probably be based on this game and how you react."

This was my chance.

Though our team was outmatched, losing 34-16, I threw for nearly 300 yards and a touchdown, and also rushed for about 40 yards and another score. I had one of my best games ever. I put on a show that night. And finally, for once, my stats were better than Ronald's.

As my senior year approached, Coach Reamon oversaw my college recruitment and made it known that schools had to choose which quarterback they wanted—me or Ronald Curry—and that recruiting both of us simultaneously wasn't an option.

He told them, "You make that decision. Michael has been 'second fiddle' long enough. He's not going to go to a place that Ronald is considering."

Once we made it to college and the pros, I caught up with Ronald. It was great to move past our rivalry and support each other in the next stage of our careers. He battled injuries at the University of North Carolina and wound up playing wide receiver in the NFL for seven seasons with the Oakland Raiders. But in high school, I remained in his shadow as he led his Hampton High teams to three state championships and beat my team three consecutive seasons.

After his senior season, Ronald was named National Player of the Year by Gatorade and the Atlanta Touchdown Club. He was honored as a first-team *Parade* All-American and as the McDonald's National Player of the Year in basketball. He was every school's prized recruit in the Class of '98.

For four years, I was second-best. But it made me want to be the best—the best ever.

Chapter Three

Blacksburg's a Blast

"This is it. This is all I ever dreamed of."

E verything changed in college. I was no longer living in another quarterback's shadow. My career launched.

I was being recruited by schools all across the country, but I narrowed it to five for my official visits: Clemson, East Carolina, Georgia Tech, Syracuse, and Virginia Tech. Going on all of my official visits and seeing different campuses was a great experience for me at the time. Aside from traveling to high school games and football camps, visiting the schools took me out of Newport News and showed me so much of what I never knew. Life was definitely different away from Newport News.

The visits provided Coach Reamon and me an opportunity to evaluate all of my options and the possible scenarios that were ahead. Clemson wanted me to come in and play immediately as a true freshman, whereas Georgia Tech had a standout quarterback, Joe Hamilton, who had two years remaining. I definitely didn't want to wait that long. And East Carolina was moving to Conference USA and had a freshman quarterback named David

Garrard already waiting in the wings. In the end, it came down to Syracuse and Virginia Tech, two schools that were in the Big East Conference.

Coach Reamon urged me to attend Virginia Tech. The Hokies were nearby and also were willing to allow me to redshirt my first season in order to develop as a player before competing for the starting quarterback position. This would be a great chance for me to sit back, learn, and adjust to college.

The same opportunity was available at Syracuse because Donovan McNabb—whose career has been closely linked to mine—was entering his senior season. Donovan hosted my campus visit to Syracuse and hoped to convince me to join the Orangemen. He said I became his "little brother" during the recruiting process.

For some reason, our paths have always seemed to be intertwined. In 2010, Donovan was traded to the Washington Redskins after eleven incredible seasons with the Philadelphia Eagles. He was the starting quarterback for the Monday night game in November 2010 that my Eagles won, 59-21. During his tenure in Philadelphia, Donovan and the Eagles beat my Atlanta Falcons team twice in the playoffs, ending some exciting seasons for us.

Donovan is a great player and an underappreciated quarterback. More importantly, he has been a great trailblazer for other African-American quarterbacks, redefining the role and image with the likes of Doug Williams and Randall Cunningham. If not for Donovan, I might not have been signed by the Eagles when I was seeking reentry into the NFL, nor would I have been so well-mentored in my first year back. He played a huge part in getting me signed in Philadelphia and in my rehabilitation as a football player. But our friendship began not in the NFL, but on my recruiting trip to Syracuse.

I had a great time on that official visit. Donovan was a terrific host. We went to a Syracuse basketball game together at the Carrier Dome. But Syracuse also had twelve inches of snow on the ground with single-digit temperatures, and I was a ten-hour drive away from home. That let me know it would be tough for my family to get there on a consistent basis to see me play, which was important to me.

So it was either go play at Syracuse and fill Donovan McNabb's shoes, or go to Virginia Tech and create my own legacy. Both seemed like a challenge and a good opportunity, but I believed in myself and really wanted to mark my place in college football history. I knew I could do it.

I prayed about the decision. I asked God to guide me, and it became clear that Tech was the right choice. I loved the idea of playing for Coach Frank Beamer, who impressed me not only as an excellent coach but as a highly admirable person I could respect and follow as a leader. He was like a father away from home for all of his players. I was a kid coming from a completely different environment—not used to being away from home—and I clung to him and picked his brain about different situations in regards to growing up and becoming a man. He helped me adjust to the college environment and told my mother he would take care of me.

When I went to Tech, I wasn't thinking about what I needed to do to put the program on the map; all I was concerned about was winning football games.

I knew it wasn't going to be easy adjusting to both the playing level of Division 1-A (now Bowl Championship Series) college football and the college atmosphere in general—going to class, being responsible, and living a totally different life. The academic side demanded so much more than high school; that alone would be a challenge for me. Then add the life of a college football player—practicing three hours a day, lifting weights for about two hours a day, and traveling most weekends.

Plus, if I wanted to attain my college football dreams—well, I had *a lot* to learn.

⌇

The redshirt year is invaluable. Many parents today want their kids to play *now*. They want them to pick a college where they can play immediately.

I could have done the same thing. Believe me. I could have played right out of high school. Physically, I certainly could.

Football, however, isn't about what you can do physically. A running back, for example, also has to know how to block. He has to know what to do against a full blitz or an assigned linebacker. It's not *just* about taking the handoff and shaking the guys in front of you. It's about routes. It's about coverage conversions.

The game is first played from a mental standpoint—then the physical. Without the mental, you don't know where to go. All you are is a good football player—with no knowledge—so what good are you? You're just sitting there like a bump on a log because you don't know what to do. You're nothing but wasted talent because you don't know how to think and process. A redshirt season will help you maximize your opportunity to go to the next level.

Virginia Tech kept its promise to Coach Reamon and me: they gave me the opportunity to sit my true freshman season. They had a good football team and senior quarterback Al Clark, so I think they felt like they could hold on for a year without playing me, and it paid off. I really wanted things to be in perspective before I started playing regularly—to understand the game. I wanted to mature and make sure I was ready to handle everything.

Physically, I improved exponentially. I had never gone through anything like the regimen they provided. It was hard, but so rewarding. I went from being just a fast player to having elite speed that is said to be unparalleled at the quarterback position. I also gained about twenty pounds, increasing from 190 to 210.

The difference? Lifting weights. It was all muscle. It's what happens when you lift three times a day.

Tech had a weight room as big as a hotel ballroom. Between the squats, clean and press, and bench, I was doing leg weights and upper-body weights in addition to drinking protein shakes and eating three square meals a day in the cafeteria. As a result, I just took off as my physique matured.

Most importantly, I improved mentally. Our offensive coordinator and quarterbacks coach, Rickey Bustle, always made me come to the film room. Practice didn't start until 3:30 p.m., but I was in quarterback meetings at 2:00 p.m. When the other redshirts were out socializing and starting their weekend, I was in the film room with Rickey. The playbook was thicker, and there were defensive concepts I hadn't seen in high school. I had to learn. They had plans for me to play. And they were going to make sure I was mentally prepared.

The first thing to being a good quarterback, you see, isn't about learning the offense, believe it or not. It's about learning how to read defenses.

All through summer camp my redshirt season, I looked lost in practice. Even through the regular season, I looked lost. But I'll never forget it: I was sitting in the film room before our bowl game—the Music City Bowl against Alabama—studying and watching film. That's when it clicked.

Cover 1, you can do *xyz*.

Cover 2, you can do *xyz*.

For each defense, I finally understood the things I could do. And that was pretty much the game. Up until then, it was all cloudy; I didn't understand. From that point forward, going against the scout team, I looked for two high safeties or a single-high safety, and I read the defense. From that point forward, all I had to do was learn the offense because I had already learned the defense.

Between my physical and mental maturation, coaches told me I started to look like the best scout-team player to ever play the game. I learned how to be a leader. I learned how to be the best. And it all came down to that day in the film room when it clicked.

It's when my raw abilities came to fruition because they were combined with a refined physical and mental game. It's when it started to show.

⌐⌐

During the spring of my redshirt freshman season, I was competing with junior Dave Meyer for the starting quarterback position. I had an opportunity to lead the team come fall if I earned the position in spring practice. Virginia Tech could be *my* team. My college football dreams could become a reality.

I'll never forget the day I found out I was No. 1 on the depth chart.

I spent January, February, and March learning the offense. And on the first day of spring practice, I put everything I learned together. In the fall, I had felt lost. But now, the game felt easy.

Dave and I started out dead even. We each had two weeks with the first-string offense and two weeks with the second-string. We had full practices on Saturday and were evaluated on Sundays.

On one of those Saturdays, I remember going 8-for-10 with 133 passing yards. I specifically remember a touchdown pass I had to our tight end on a broken-arrow route against a cover 3 defense— which was rare. But because of my vision, I saw it in the drop back.

That night, I went home to Newport News. People don't realize this, but I used to get incredibly homesick. It felt so good to see my family, and when I came back for practice, I had completely forgotten about the depth chart. When I saw it, I got butterflies: "Vick— No. 1, Meyer—No. 2." The first person I called was my mom.

And instantly, my team started looking at me like I was a leader—*their* leader.

By the time it was my turn to play as a redshirt freshman in 1999, my skills had improved dramatically. I was faster than everyone, and quicker too. My athletic talent could still take over, but now I had a greater knowledge of the game from a cerebral perspective. I learned to make better decisions on each play, and how to make good decisions on broken plays as well.

My college debut came against James Madison on September 4, 1999, and I was literally unleashed to the college football world.

I had butterflies like never before. All week long, I was asking my teammates questions about what to expect:

"What's it like being out there on the field?"

"What's it like playing college football?"

This was my dream. I was nervous.

"You'll be fine," they told me.

"You'll be all right."

"You're fast," a teammate said. "You're the fastest dude out there. You'll be fine."

"No, you don't understand," I replied. "This is my *first game*. So what if you see me breaking thirty-yard runs in practice? That's practice—"

"Yeah, but you're practicing against a great Virginia Tech defense," he said.

On the thirty-minute bus ride from the hotel to the game, I fell asleep. It was only a half hour, but it felt like a two-hour nap. We got to the stadium, and there were people everywhere. I can't explain the way I felt.

I remember going to the locker room, getting changed, and standing in the tunnel repeating to myself, *This is it. This is it. This is it.*

I touched our good-luck charm, a rock. *I'm gonna need it*, I said to myself.

Standing in that tunnel, all I could think about was my mother. No matter what happened in that game, I knew it wouldn't affect the way she felt about me. I was still going to be her baby; I was still going to get that kiss from her after the game. In her eyes, nothing would change about me. It helped settle my nerves.

We ended up getting the ball first. *Of course*, I thought to myself. *Just my luck.*

Jogging onto the field, I looked up to the sky. It was a bright, sunny day. *Here we go*, I said to myself. *Here we go.*

At that point, my biggest battle was mental. I knew I had the abilities. *I know what to do*, I told myself. *I've studied James Madison to a T. I know what they're going to try to do.*

Before I knew it, I was in the huddle. The first play I called was a pass play—deep comebacks against a single high, meaning you can throw to the comebacks outside. There was a guy wide open downfield. But I was so nervous, instead of throwing to the guy downfield, I threw a flat route. And not just that, but I threw it into the dirt.

The whole stadium grew silent. They saw how wide open the receiver was. They saw how I messed up.

After punting on our first drive, we turned it around. I scored on a 3-yard run on our second possession. On our third drive, I called a quarterback draw on second and six. The play was called "Bronco Joe." I took a three-step drop, then went up the middle. Next thing I knew, I was by myself, running into the end zone for a 54-yard touchdown.

This is kind of cool, I said to myself. *I just, like, ran past everybody.*

In the second quarter we scored 12 more points, which included a 60-yard pass on one of our drives and a 7-yard touchdown run with less than nine minutes to go. Unfortunately, I never returned for the second half because I injured myself when I jumped over a guy into the end zone and fell awkwardly—spraining my ankle. (The injury also sidelined me for the next game.) But I threw for 110 yards and ran for three touchdowns in the James Madison game, a 47-0 victory. Fans said it was the best half of football they'd ever seen. And it had the whole city of Blacksburg buzzing.

My college career was really ignited in our third game that season against Clemson—when I returned from my injury. Statistically, it wasn't one of my better games. I had three interceptions—the only time in my college career. Clemson was different from James Madison. But a particular play helped my college career explode.

It was third down, 14-11 in our favor, with little time left in the fourth quarter, and Clemson had just scored 11 unanswered points. With their momentum, they would probably tie the game with a field goal or win with a touchdown if we didn't convert a first down. I stepped up to the line of scrimmage. Scanning the field, I saw my tight end against a cover 3 defense and an out-of-place linebacker. Typically, throwing to your tight end against that type of defense is a no-no. But I saw it, went against my rules, made the throw with confidence, and completed a first down. We ended up scoring 17 points to close out the game and win 31-11.

My coach later told me, "A quarterback who was rattled, scared, or not sure of himself never would have made that play in a clutch moment."

Our game at Rutgers in week five became a considerable break-out game that propelled me into the Heisman Trophy conversation, and our biggest win in 1999 came in the regular season finale against No. 22-ranked Boston College.

I'll never forget the way the clouds looked that day against Boston College. It was raining, it was cloudy, but the sun was peeking through. The game meant everything to us because it was an opportunity to secure our spot in the BCS National Championship.

I went out and played an almost perfect game. I passed for three touchdowns and nearly 300 yards, and rushed for 70-plus yards and another score in a 38-14 victory. I'll never forget my teammates carrying me off the field after we had accomplished our goal, which was to go 11-0 and earn the right to play for a national championship. My teammates and I put ourselves in a position to take the team where we wanted to go.

We were headed to the national championship game.

I was flying. In high school, perhaps I was still learning the purpose behind my wings. I knew I had them. But there were others who were better. There were others, like Ronald Curry, who had seemingly more promising futures. But after redshirting my first year at Virginia Tech—working, building, learning how to utilize my skills—I was prepared for takeoff. Now, I was in flight. And all I wanted to do was fly higher . . . and higher . . . and higher.

In a way, the year was a landmark season for Virginia Tech—putting the program, the school, and me on the national map. I had one of the best seasons of any player in the country, completing 58 percent of my passes for 2,000-plus yards and thirteen touchdowns, and also rushing for nearly 700 yards and nine more scores in eleven games.

My life was changing. I received awards—a lot of awards. I was mentioned in the national press. My highlights were on ESPN. My name was everywhere. Two years before, I was second to Ronald Curry. Not now. All of the big dreams Coach Reamon encouraged me to dream became realities.

On the other side of things—the personal side—it was difficult. I wasn't used to signing autographs. I would walk around on campus and people would scream my name—then approach me requesting my signature. When I walked into class, everyone stared at me and wanted to talk to me. Everyone wanted to be my friend. Everyone wanted a piece of me. I had no idea that good performances on the field could bring about friendships and fame.

When I was a kid watching the NFL on television, I saw the fame and fortune of guys like Emmitt Smith, Steve Young, Troy Aikman, and Brett Favre, but I didn't know what came along with it. I solely dreamed of being a good football player. That's all. I didn't understand the concept of signing autographs—didn't even think about it. You can't prepare for that. And it was overwhelming.

In December I finished third in the Heisman Trophy voting with 319 points, behind winner Ron Dayne (Wisconsin running back, 2,042 points) and Joe Hamilton (Georgia Tech quarterback, 994 points). I finished just ahead of NFL peers Drew Brees (Purdue quarterback, 308 points) and Chad Pennington (Marshall quarterback, 247 points).

After the new year I traveled to New Orleans with Tech to play Florida State in the 2000 BCS Nokia Sugar Bowl, the year's national championship game between the top two teams in the BCS poll. I was only nineteen years old on the biggest stage of college football, and more than eighteen million people were watching.

Walking onto the field was a surreal feeling. Ever since I was a kid, I had dreamed of that moment and tried to imagine that feeling. To be playing in that game and living in that moment was almost incomprehensible. I remember taking the first snap and realizing, *This is my dream—playing in a national championship.*

The first five minutes of the game, I didn't even know where I was. I couldn't wrap my mind around it. And after the first few possessions, I had a headache because the crowd was so loud. I couldn't hear my teammates and had to scream at the top of my lungs in the huddle. I eventually settled down and zoned in on the task at hand.

We started off slow and trailed 28-7 late in the second quarter, but we clawed back and took a 29-28 lead at the start of the fourth.

In the fourth, however, Florida State scored 18 unanswered points to win the title, 49-26. I played well, passing for over 200 yards and a touchdown and rushing for nearly 100 yards and a touchdown, but I would trade playing well for a win or title any day.

After the game, I reflected on what it took to get there—how my teammates and I had gone undefeated to put Virginia Tech football on the map; yet in the end, we lost. I was upset, but I was also confident that the following year, we'd once again have a chance to win. I had to be happy with what we accomplished—an 11-1 season, the best in Hokies history.

After the season, ESPN invited me to the 2000 ESPYs—the annual gala honoring excellence in sports—in Las Vegas, Nevada. It seemed so far from Ridley Park's unit 667 in Newport News. ESPN named me the National Player of the Year for college football.

I never really thought I would be on that big a stage. I took my mom with me, and the experience meant a lot to us. It was a chance for me to take her somewhere nice like she did so many times for me when I was a kid. It gave us some quality time. She had the chance to meet many famous athletes, like Peyton Manning and Michael Jordan. It was awesome for us to experience the event after everything we'd gone through in life—how hard she had worked to take care of our family and how hard I had worked to get where I was. I thought to myself, *You're almost there, but you still have a lot of work to do to achieve greatness.*

My redshirt freshman season in 1999 catapulted me to a level far beyond what I had anticipated, and it raised expectations for my sophomore season that would be difficult to reach.

The loss in the Sugar Bowl left me hungry to accomplish more as a sophomore. I worked extremely hard during spring practices. I also spent a lot of time in the weight room, which helped me get stronger and even faster (I ran a 4.25 forty-yard dash in spring testing, the second-fastest time in school history). One memorable moment in the weight room was in June, just prior to the beginning of preseason camp. I was lifting, and some of my teammates came in and said that they had seen on *SportsCenter* that I was selected by the Colorado Rockies as the 887th overall pick of the Major League Baseball draft. I didn't really believe them at first; I couldn't believe someone was interested in *me* playing baseball. But when I found out it was true, I thought it was pretty cool. I hadn't even played baseball since I was in the eighth grade, other than practicing a little with the team at Warwick during my senior year of high school. The whole situation just showed that people recognized my athleticism.

As the 2000 season approached, it seemed as though I was on the cover of every magazine in the country. I was gaining popularity and receiving all types of national exposure. There was so much hype around me and the Hokies, and we had a great team returning with an explosive offense. We were loaded with Lee Suggs at running back, along with wide receivers André Davis and my former Warwick High teammate, Andrae Harrison. The only thing I wanted was to achieve at the highest level. I really wanted to win a national championship, but I also desired the Heisman Trophy so I could bring it back to my Newport News neighborhood.

I don't know if I can fully explain the Heisman hype and the pressure that came with it. The Department of Athletics at Virginia Tech created a special website tracking my performances and the Heisman race. They developed a huge PR campaign supporting me, which I was grateful for, but I can't say that it didn't become a distraction and add pressure.

Our season started well. We won our first eight games and climbed to No. 2 in the AP and, most importantly, BCS polls. We were getting close to playing for the national title again. Late in the season against unranked Pittsburgh, however, I suffered a high-ankle sprain that limited me the remainder of the season. I sprained my ankle during the second quarter, trying to stay back and make a big play when I could have easily made it downfield for a shorter gain. My team stepped up big-time and won the game, 37-34.

The injury ended up eliminating me from the Heisman race. I wanted to win the Heisman, not for myself, but for Newport News. Bringing that trophy back to my city was the dream that fueled me. I was just a kid with dreams, who grew up in poverty like so many others there. I wanted to bring it back. I wanted to be an encouragement to others in the city that I loved. The opportunity was right there, and something that I couldn't control—an injury—prevented me from seizing it.

I'm convinced that the injury happened because I lost sight of what was important. I was consumed with the Heisman race, and my focus was on me. I was still concerned with the team, but I also entered each game knowing that I had to produce stats and be efficient. I put a tremendous amount of pressure on myself to play above expectations, lead my team, and win the Heisman Trophy. I was at a point where the pressure affected my play; I was playing hesitantly and indecisively and was afraid to make mistakes.

The injury severely limited me in the biggest game of the year—November 4, 2000, against Miami—when we were ranked No. 2 in the country and they were No. 3. The winner would most likely take the Big East crown and potentially the conference's BCS berth in the national championship game: the 2001 FedEx Orange Bowl.

I was day-to-day all week prior, spent a good deal of time in a special Fortis Brace, and was a game-time decision. I didn't start the game, but attempted to play after we fell behind. I lasted only nineteen snaps. I gave it my best shot and tried to be there for my team, but I just couldn't do it. I wouldn't take the pain-killing shot, which would've numbed me, potentially allowing me to play some more (I'm afraid of needles). Plus, I felt it would be selfish to go out and play. I thought I would be hurting my teammates more than helping them.

All I could do in the second half was watch as we went on to lose 41-21, essentially ending our national title hopes. It was excruciating being unable to play in a game that I still believe we would have won if I'd been healthy. Every year, it seemed, an injury slowed me down.

After the loss, the Heisman talk mostly ended. Though that was disappointing, it may have helped me play better in the final game of the season and our bowl game. It was like the weight of the whole world was lifted off my shoulders. We beat Virginia 42-21 to close out the regular season and then defeated Clemson 41-20 in the Gator Bowl, where I was named the game's MVP.

We again finished 11-1 and were ranked No. 6 and No. 5 nationally in the final AP and BCS polls, respectively. I finished the season with a 54.2 completion percentage, passing for about 1,500 yards and nine touchdowns while rushing for nearly 700 yards and nine touchdowns.

As for the Heisman, I finished sixth in the voting. Chris Weinke, the quarterback at Florida State, won the honor. Future NFL players Drew Brees and LaDainian Tomlinson finished third and fourth in the voting.

Though I had two years of college eligibility remaining, I began weighing the possibility of turning pro, especially since there was word that I could be the first overall pick in the NFL draft—something that had never before happened for an African-American quarterback.

It was a tough decision. I had become so accustomed to living a balanced life at Virginia Tech. I was having a blast; I was on my own, in control of my life and career, and in charge of the offense at one of the top collegiate programs in the country, which had contended for the national championship the last two seasons.

I knew moving to the NFL would mean greater responsibility. Even though there would be no schoolwork involved, there would be more of a need to dedicate myself to perfecting my craft on the football field, and there would be more pressure to win games. I knew all the things that came along with playing professional football; I just didn't know if I was responsible enough to do those things, and if I was ready for it. But as time went on and I saw the opportunity present itself, along with the potential to go No. 1, it seemed that everything I wanted was right there in front of me.

But it was hard because I would have to tell my coaches and my mom that I was going to leave Virginia Tech. When I finally made my decision, I had an emotional conversation with Coach Beamer. He called me and told me, "Regardless of what you do, I'm going to support you . . . to the very last day." Coach was crying on the phone, and I had tears in my eyes. I told him, "Coach, I'm leaving. I have to do it, not only for myself but for my family."

It was one of the toughest decisions I'd had to make at that point in my life. I was used to being around Coach Beamer and my teammates—it was comfortable. The Virginia Tech program provided a family atmosphere, and they had given me the opportunity to come and run the program. They put all their trust in me. Virginia Tech meant a great deal to me, so leaving was a very hard thing to do.

$$\smile$$

It was difficult to leave Tech and turn pro because I had not yet received my college degree, which was important to me and my family—especially my mother. I left school with fewer than forty credit hours remaining (I think thirty-six, to be exact) to qualify for graduation. I promised my mom I would eventually go back to school to complete my studies and earn my degree.

Contrary to what some people may think, I actually did enjoy school. When I entered college, I really wanted to study criminology, but that wasn't offered as a major at Tech. Ironic as it may sound, I desired to work in forensics—to do undercover work—after my football career was over. I decided to major in sociology instead.

I was not the best student; I was just average. But I gave a good effort. I took advantage of the academic support the Hokies provided: I went to study hall, and I met with all my tutors. I am proud to say that my academic eligibility and standing were never in question. I probably could have performed better in the classroom, but the fact was that football took up a lot of my time, even though I do not want to use that as an excuse.

I have fond memories of the people who supported my studies at school—my professors, tutors, and advisors. But one person who really stood out was my favorite professor, Nikki Giovanni from the English department. She was an accomplished poet, a published author, and an expert in African studies. Everyone who had her as a teacher really enjoyed her classes. I had a deep love and appreciation for her and how well she was able to teach and keep her students engaged. It was cool because a lot of my teammates and I were in her class together, and we were able to learn from her as a team.

One of Professor Giovanni's famous quotes is this: "Everything will change. The only question is [whether it's] growing up or decaying."

The choice was mine.

Coach Beamer joined my mother and me at the Boys & Girls Club in Newport News for the press conference on January 11, 2001, announcing my decision to turn pro.

I almost didn't make the deadline to enter the draft for underclassmen because the NFL does not accept fax copies of transcripts—they require original copies. Two days before the deadline, we boarded a small, private plane to travel from the Hampton, Virginia, area to Roanoke. We then drove to the Tech campus in Blacksburg to pick up my college transcripts so they would make it to the NFL office on time. It was a close call. I made it nonetheless.

The day I announced my decision to turn pro was an emotional time for all of us. Coach Beamer knew what type of environment I came from because he had visited me two or three times at my house in Ridley Circle. So he understood how incredible it was for me to have a chance to play in the NFL and to earn a significant income for my family and me.

Coach Beamer meant the world to me—and still does to this day. He's a great man whose principles are valuable far beyond the playing field. Coach Beamer reiterates this phrase so much: "You've got to do things the right way." It sticks in your mind and it gets embedded in your heart—that you've got to do things the right way. It's what he teaches in his program, and that's a quality you can carry into your life after football.

I wish I had heeded that principle more in the years that followed. Like Professor Giovanni's quote says, everything changes. Surroundings change. Situations change. And in change—in transition—you can change for the better, or you can change for the worse.

I was flying. The landscape below was changing.

I would either grow up, or I would decay.

Chapter Four
Favorite Falcon

"I could have done more."

The moment I announced my decision, my life changed forever. I was leaving behind all that I knew and had become accustomed to—leaving the nest. There was no turning back; I felt I was ready to spread my wings and fly even higher than before.

The cast around me was changing. The landscape below was changing. There was no more Coach Beamer, Tech support staff, or anything like that. I had my friends, my marketing reps, and my agents. People were coming at me from all over the place to be in the "Business of Michael Vick." There was a lot happening around me, and all I wanted was to get drafted. I was a kid. I wasn't even twenty-one years old.

For me, the whole draft process began when I was invited to attend the annual NFL Scouting Combine in Indianapolis. Elite players from across the country are selected by NFL general managers and other executives to attend the combine. The players are put through a series of physical tests, medical exams, football drills, psychological evaluations, and interviews with team personnel.

I chose not to participate in many of the activities at the combine. But I did sit for all of the exams and interviews, which I believe went really well. I waited until my Pro Day at Virginia Tech to show my athletic abilities. Pro Days are held by college football programs to showcase their prospects' talent to NFL scouts. Essentially, they are mini-combines held on campus for NFL teams to attend if they want.

I was a little nervous that morning in March when my Pro Day arrived, but in the end, I tore it up. I ran the forty-yard dash in 4.33 seconds, a speed unmatched by any other quarterback. More importantly though, I performed at an extremely high level in the football drills; I don't know if I could have done better than I did. I think I completed all but one of my throws, putting only one ball on the ground. My accuracy was on, and my velocity was excellent as well. My arm felt strong, and I was throwing hard—so hard, in fact, that I broke one of my receiver's fingers with a pass. In addition to that, my timing was on. I was putting it all together: accuracy, velocity, timing, and footwork.

I felt great after my Pro Day; I was full of confidence. I felt like I put in strong performances at my individual workouts with the teams too. What I had accomplished made me feel like the top prospect for the draft. In reality, I didn't care if I was the first pick in the first round or the third pick in the third round; I just wanted the opportunity to play professional football.

Just like the prior year, I had become a national story and was on the cover of *ESPN The Magazine.* Every football pundit on television was talking about me during predraft coverage on CBS, NBC, ESPN, etc.; some of the talk was positive, some was negative, and some of it just raised questions.

A few experts had the opportunity to share their thoughts with *Sports Illustrated.*

Former New York Giants Super Bowl-winning quarterback Phil Simms was quoted as saying, "The real question you have to ask yourself is whether any person in this draft can change your franchise. There's one: Michael Vick."

James Harris, the director of pro personnel for the Baltimore Ravens at the time, said, "He could well become one of the greatest playmakers in NFL history."

But on the flip side, Hall of Fame coach Bill Walsh—the 49ers vice president and GM at the time—said, "He has more potential than [Drew] Brees, but I don't see how he'll be able to play regularly until his third year."

Some people said I wouldn't stay healthy or play for long, given my penchant for running and throwing my body around; plus, I was considered small. They also questioned whether I could transfer my skills and the excitement I brought in college to the NFL.

All of it was talk. I just wanted to start my professional career.

The San Diego Chargers had the first pick in the 2001 draft and were widely expected to pick me as they looked to rebuild their franchise, but they had been burned by quarterback Ryan Leaf, a major bust. In the buildup to the draft, the Chargers waived Leaf and traded their No. 1 selection to the Atlanta Falcons just one day before the draft. In exchange, Atlanta gave San Diego their first-round choice (No. 5 overall), a third-round pick, a 2002 second-round selection, plus veteran wide receiver/kick returner Tim Dwight.

At the time, I thought that was an odd trade. I felt like my visit with the Chargers had gone well, and I knew they had some pre-liminary contract talks with my agents. I also knew they were looking for a quarterback and maybe a running back.

I later heard that the Chargers made the trade because they became uncomfortable with drafting me. I had brought friends with me to a workout—friends they didn't trust would be positive influences in my life—thus making me too great a risk for them to take with the top pick.

I acknowledge that showing up with friends for my workout was very unprofessional. I've heard it said that the world is 90 percent perception and 10 percent reality. I'd agree. The Chargers didn't know my friends. They may have actually been good people, but the Chargers automatically assumed that those weren't the right people to have around because of the image and persona they projected.

In the big picture though, I was actually ecstatic about the trade because it worked in my favor. I didn't want to go all the way out to California and leave my family. Atlanta was a one-hour flight away, and an eight-hour drive by car, and I love driving. So if I went as the first pick, it was perfect for me.

Around the time of the draft, I had the opportunity to meet two of my quarterbacking heroes who, like me, had nimble feet to go with strong arms: Steve Young and Randall Cunningham. I was very flattered that Young said he believed I had once-in-a-generation potential. The admiration was entirely mutual.

Young was my favorite player growing up because, like me, he was a lefty and a runner. He played for the San Francisco 49ers, and I loved him with the 49ers. He had all types of weapons around him—Jerry Rice, John Taylor, Ricky Watters—and Deion Sanders was there a couple of years too. The defense had Ken Norton, Merton Hanks, Tim McDonald, Eric Davis, and Charles Haley. They were stacked!

I always dreamed of being the leader of a team like that.

The day of the draft was beautiful. It was a perfect spring day in New York City, and I just knew I would be the first pick. I had been waiting for this day since I was seven years old—when I told my grandmother that I wanted to play professional football and she looked at me and said, "Well, you have to learn how to play."

And here I was.

At the draft, I was with my mom, dad, brother, both sisters, two close friends, cousins, and my then-girlfriend and high school sweetheart, Tameka Taylor. We were really excited because we knew going to the NFL would be a life-changing situation.

Shortly after the draft began, I watched as then-NFL commissioner Paul Tagliabue stepped up to the podium and said, "With the first selection in the 2001 NFL draft, the Atlanta Falcons select Michael Vick, quarterback, Virginia Tech." I was beyond emotion. I hugged everyone I was with. Then I walked onto the stage of the theater at Madison Square Garden, shook hands with the commissioner, and was handed an Atlanta Falcons hat and a jersey with No. 1 on it, just like high school—only this time I knew I would only wear No. 7. I couldn't keep the smile off my face. I was an Atlanta Falcon.

I was headed to a talented team. They had a veteran quarterback I could learn from in Chris Chandler, Pro Bowl running back Jamal Anderson, and talented receivers Terance Mathis and Tony Martin. On defense, there were up-and-coming youngsters Keith Brooking and Patrick Kerney. It was a great situation.

Not only had I become an NFL quarterback and the second No. 1 pick from Virginia Tech (Bruce Smith, 1985), most importantly, I was the first African-American quarterback in history to be picked first overall in the NFL draft.

It was, and still is, a tremendous honor. It's something that will stand forever—the first one. I was the first to overcome that barrier in African-American history. Others, like Donovan McNabb, were capable, but I don't think it was ever a racial thing. Teams pick based on their needs. Since then, two more black quarterbacks have been drafted first overall: LSU's JaMarcus Russell in

2007 by the Oakland Raiders, and Auburn's Cam Newton in 2011 by the Carolina Panthers.

⌒

The trade worked out not only for me and the Falcons, but for the Chargers too. Some commentators, like *Sports Illustrated*'s Peter King, have since said it was the most interesting trade of the decade. San Diego picked TCU running back LaDainian Tomlinson with the fifth selection and used their second-round pick on Purdue quarterback Drew Brees, giving them a sensational—even historic—draft and the position players they needed. Tomlinson and Brees teamed up to make San Diego a consistent contender and one of the most talented teams in the NFL.

LaDainian, who moved to the New York Jets through free agency before the 2010-11 season, has had a Hall of Fame career. Drew might also be en route to enshrinement in Canton, Ohio, especially after leading the New Orleans Saints to a Super Bowl championship and earning MVP honors in the process.

The Falcons, then owned by Taylor Smith, made the 2001 trade expecting great things from me. In an interview shortly after the trade, Atlanta's general manager at the time, Harold Richardson, told *Sports Illustrated*'s Don Banks that he considered the swap comparable to the deal the Denver Broncos made to acquire quarterback John Elway from the then-Baltimore Colts in 1983. Elway eventually led the Broncos to two Super Bowl titles and three other championship game appearances in a Hall of Fame career.

My first coach in Atlanta, Dan Reeves, says that back then he thought I could be a player similar to Elway, my childhood idol Steve Young, or former Dallas Cowboys great Roger Staubach. Reeves coached Elway, coached against Young, and played with Staubach. All of those quarterbacks were good runners, great leaders, Super Bowl champions, and league MVPs. Coach Reeves thought I was a good scrambler and would only get better as I "learned to throw the football and not rely on running so much." He later said, "I don't know of anybody who ever played the game that—at the quarterback position—was the fastest player on the field."

But in addition to my playing ability, the Falcons drafted me to rebrand the franchise and help sell tickets. Anytime you've got a team that's struggling, you want to bring in a main attraction. Maybe LaDainian Tomlinson would've done it too, but Atlanta already had a top running back in Jamal Anderson. I was ready to bring excitement to Atlanta.

⌒⌒

My first contract dramatically changed my economic base, filling my bank account with more money than I'd ever fathomed growing up in Newport News. That in itself was a huge challenge as I adjusted to the NFL.

My $3 million signing bonus was my first paycheck in the NFL, but after taxes, it ended up being about $1.9 million. I was surprised by the taxes taken out of my check.

No one taught me how to handle money. I never had a real job. I had been active in sports as a youngster, so the only paying jobs I had before the NFL were working part-time as a painter for my uncle and serving as a pool boy for my high school coach.

In addition to being naïve about taxes, I was not prepared to go from having no money in my pocket to $2 million. Suddenly, I could buy my mom everything I promised her and everything I wanted for her. I could buy almost anything. The world was mine.

The first thing I bought was a gold Lincoln Navigator with 22-inch rims. My second purchase was four scooters. And my third purchase was my mother's house. It felt great to be able to buy my mom whatever she wanted. I felt like she had been a part of everything I worked for.

As a family, we knew we would be set financially for the rest of our lives. It was complete jubilation. But we also knew that with more money came more responsibility for me, and I wanted to do a lot of things for my family. I gave everyone a nice chunk of change—$20,000 or $30,000 apiece. I took care of a lot of people because we had a very tight-knit family and we stuck together. We were there for one another.

I put my family in the position to go out and buy themselves nice things and live comfortably. It was gratifying, and I enjoyed providing for them—even spoiling them.

I was very blessed that my arrival in Atlanta seemed to infuse excitement into the Falcons' organization. Ticket sales escalated, and the team's value was on the rise by the time Taylor Smith sold the franchise to Home Depot cofounder Arthur Blank in 2002.

I had a positive public image for my first four or five seasons in the NFL. Our team made two playoff appearances, including a berth in the NFC Championship game during the 2004 season, and I was selected to three Pro Bowls.

I played sparingly as a rookie, starting only twice, and passing for two touchdowns and running for one. A rushing touchdown was the first score of my pro career. It happened in the second game of the season against the Carolina Panthers.

We were on the 2-yard line, and I can remember approaching the end zone. The Panthers had their backs turned, and I was saying to myself, *There is the end zone right there. Just get to it.* I took off.

Panthers safety Mike Minter turned around quickly—at the drop of a dime—and hit me right in the ribs. I still made it to the end zone, which made me happy. But at the same time, I was hurting because he bruised my ribs. The play was just like when I scored my first Pop Warner touchdown as a quarterback: I was on the ground. After I stood up, all I could think was, *That's the first of many.*

We finished 7-9 my rookie year. But we improved to 9-6-1 and earned a wildcard berth to the playoffs the next season as I became the full-time starter and the face of the franchise. We got off to a slow start at 1-3, but then completed an NFL-best, eight-game unbeaten streak, going 7-0-1 during the stretch.

In September of that same season, I was blessed to return to Blacksburg, where Virginia Tech honored me by retiring my jersey. I became the fifth player in school history to receive such an honor.

The moment was particularly special because it was something I never included in my dreams of becoming an NFL quarterback. More than anything, it showed me that I was on the right track. Here I was—just a kid from Newport News who had a dream of being an NFL player—and my college jersey was being retired after only two seasons on the field with the Hokies and one year in the NFL. It gave me a huge confidence boost for my second NFL season—my first as Atlanta's regular starter.

It was a different atmosphere from my rookie year to my second year. Though I approached playing in the NFL with a relaxed and mellow attitude since we were rebuilding and flying under the radar, I still knew I had to live up to Atlanta's expectations of me. After all, they traded to get the No. 1 pick in the draft and select *me*. I had too much pride to be a draft bust.

The more games we won my second year, the more I felt like I was becoming a leader. I believe you can't make yourself a leader— people have to see leadership in you. I tried to lead by my actions on the field, and my teammates started to respect me and look to me. We had momentum heading into the playoffs, which created more of a demand for consistency. People saw our potential, so we had to live up to it.

At the age of twenty-two, I faced off against the Green Bay Packers and already-legendary quarterback Brett Favre in the wildcard game. The Packers had never lost a home playoff game at Lambeau Field, or in their earlier days in Milwaukee, going 13-0 dating back to 1933.

I can vividly remember being out there on the field during warm-ups. The snow was gently falling. There was no wind, and it was cold, but not too cold. There was an eerie feeling in the air that something special was going to happen that night.

We were happy that we made it to the playoffs. For us, that was overachieving. We knew we could play with any team in the league, but really, we didn't stack up that well with some teams, like Green Bay. We were big underdogs heading into the game, but we played exemplary football that night. Right from the beginning, we could tell it was going to be special. We scored on the opening drive—something Green Bay hadn't given up all year—en route to a 27-7 upset win.

It was Favre's first home loss of any kind when the temperature was 34 degrees or below. In a very uncharacteristic move, he didn't talk to the media after the game.

My statistics weren't sensational—117 passing yards, one touchdown, and 64 rushing yards—but the victory was exciting beyond description, and much more important and memorable. Everything went right for us that night. It was my best moment in Atlanta.

The next week, we were matched up against my old friend Donovan McNabb and his Philadelphia Eagles. Unfortunately, we lost 20-6. But it was still a successful year—even a surprising year. We flew under the radar and accomplished things that people didn't expect.

Individually, I had a solid season and was selected by my peers and the fans to go to my first Pro Bowl. I was happy. I felt like my career was headed in a good direction—up.

⌒

After all the success in 2002—the eight-game unbeaten streak to finish the season, the upset against Green Bay at Lambeau, the culture change and excitement in Atlanta—2003 was a huge disappointment for both me and the organization.

My hopes of building on 2002 ended before the 2003 season began—when I broke my leg in a preseason game against the Baltimore Ravens. Sitting on the sidelines as we went 2-10 through the first twelve games was excruciating.

The preseason injury had an impact on more than just me. It exposed a lot of weaknesses in the team, and Coach Reeves was relieved of his duties three days after my return in Week 14—when we beat Carolina 20-14 at home.

Coach Reeves will always hold a special place in my heart. I remember watching him on television when I was eight or nine years old. He was in a suit, Elway was his quarterback, and he was giving Elway a hard time. I had never seen someone look so distraught and upset during good times. But now I understand. It was just him demanding greatness. I remember telling myself at the time, *If I make it to the NFL, I don't want to play for that coach right there.*

Go figure; I ended up getting drafted by him. But I loved playing for him and connected with him. Coach Reeves gave me my first set of golf clubs. He gave me advice about how to study and become a better player. I talked to Coach Reeves on a personal level more than any other coach. And I still do.

When he got fired, I felt partially guilty. I felt like I could have done more to speak up for him, but I was only twenty-two or twenty-three years old. I didn't know the business. I didn't know if Mr. Blank would listen to me. I knew things needed to change on several levels, but I didn't want to overstep my boundaries.

We finished the year with an interim head coach, Wade Phillips, and a 5-11 record. I was hoping the year was a small bump in the road for a team that was on the rise.

After the season, and three years into my professional career, the Falcons made me the NFL's highest-paid player with a $130 million contract, further testing my self-discipline and money management. Again I was in the spotlight. In addition to my new deal, I had other earnings from corporate sponsorship deals with companies like Nike, Coca-Cola, Kraft, Hasbro, and AirTran.

The team got back on track in 2004. We had a new GM, Rich McKay, and a first-year head coach, Jim Mora. Coach Mora was what I'd call a "player's coach," someone who looked out for his guys and went out of his way to cultivate relationships with them.

We started the season 4-0 and never really looked back. We finished 11-5 while earning the second seed for the NFC playoffs. I was healthy again and put up some good numbers. Even though we lost the regular season finale, we still had a lot of confidence heading into the playoffs.

We won the divisional playoff game against quarterback Marc Bulger and the St. Louis Rams; and again, we found ourselves matched up against Donovan and Philadelphia in the NFC Championship game.

I wanted to win that game. I wanted to win that game bad. On a personal level, I knew that one of us—either me or Donovan—had the opportunity to become only the third black quarterback to start in the Super Bowl. From an African-American standpoint, that was important to me.

Donovan and I didn't speak leading up to the game. But I remember talking to him on the field before the game. It was in Philadelphia, and I was all bundled up in several layers. All Donovan was wearing was a T-shirt. He looked at me and said, "You lost already."

I laughed.

"You lost already," he joked.

Perhaps he was right. We went on to lose to Donovan and Philadelphia, 27-10. Again.

Now I'm in Philly. And I can deal with the cold.

We were changing the culture of the Falcons. There was excitement in the city. Ticket sales were up. And we were becoming a prominent contender.

The Falcons were relevant again.

My endorsement career was also skyrocketing. Being a part of the Nike family was one of my coolest experiences as a young athlete. Nike represents the best—whether it was Michael Jordan, Tiger Woods, or Derek Jeter—and it was rewarding to be a part of that.

The commercials they produced were amazing, and it was weird to think that they were about *me*. One, called "The Michael Vick Experience," featured a young boy getting on a roller coaster. It was really clever. Another was a Nike Gridiron commercial, featuring Terrell Owens and me, which had some of the coolest graphics I had ever seen.

I was also honored and humbled to go on the cover of *Madden NFL 2004*. I've always been a *Madden NFL* football fan, and it was neat to work with EA Sports on my favorite game.

I was flying high in Atlanta; Atlanta loved me, and I loved Atlanta. I loved everything about it and never wanted to play anywhere else.

I loved driving on Interstate 85.

I loved all the restaurants. My two favorite places to eat were Stoney River and the Tavern at Phipps. You went to Stoney River strictly for the steak, which was outrageously good. The Tavern was known for their honey croissants and awesome fried shrimp.

I even loved just being at Lenox Square.

But most importantly, I loved all the people. Atlanta is a diverse city—a melting pot. There is so much tradition and even growth. Like the No. 7, Atlanta fit me.

During my time there, I sincerely tried to make a difference in the metro Atlanta area by reaching out to others and serving the community. Though football was keeping me busy, and the Falcons organization had us involved in the community, I felt it was very important to give from my heart to others. It was important to me because now that I had so much, I needed to share it.

I volunteered at an orphanage. It was a chance for me to love on those kids and give them hope. I also ran a Christmas toy drive for them each year that I played in Atlanta.

During that time, I didn't just try to make an impact in Atlanta; I tried to give back in Newport News too. I did a lot of work with the Boys & Girls Club in both places. As I have said earlier, the Boys & Girls Club was a great place for me to go as a kid, and it provided me with opportunities to grow. Working with the clubs allowed me to make that same positive impact on a new generation. Also, back in Virginia, I made it a priority to help feed people at the homeless shelter. I grew up around poverty and understood its impact.

But my giving wasn't limited to my time. I tried to use my financial situation to help less fortunate people as well. I bought toys, backpacks filled with school supplies, clothes, and general necessities to give away at the orphanage and homeless shelter. I also gave to my home church in Virginia.

One opportunity stands out more than any other. In 2002 Susan Bass, the Falcons' community relations director at the time, approached me about a young boy, a twelve-year-old. She shared that he was in need of a heart transplant and that his family was in a very difficult situation. She wanted to know if I would help. There was no way I wouldn't.

I briefly met the boy and his family and decided to make a considerable contribution to assist them. I didn't want the press behind it because it wasn't about that. I just wanted to give some-one a chance to live so that he could dream like I was able to dream. I wanted to have an impact on him so that he could go out and have an impact on someone else. I wanted to give him a chance so that he could give someone else a chance.

The game in Green Bay may have been my best moment, but helping that young boy's situation was my proudest.

⌐⌐

Like the 2003 season, the 2005 and 2006 seasons were frustrating, and we regressed as a team.

In 2005 we started out great, winning six of our first eight games, but then we lost six of our last eight to finish 8-8 and miss the playoffs. Oddly, though, we sent six players to the Pro Bowl, the most for the franchise since its Super Bowl season in 1998. It was my third and final Pro Bowl as a member of the Atlanta Falcons.

We started strong again in 2006, going 5-2, but then lost our next four games en route to a 7-9 record. My mounting frustrations were evident after the fourth consecutive defeat, 31-13 to the New Orleans Saints. The loss made our record 5-6 and, just as importantly, was a huge loss to one of our NFC South division rivals.

Individually, my season was going well. I was on the way to what would be one of the best statistical years of my career, with a career high in touchdown passes (20) and an NFL record for rushing yards by a quarterback (1,039). In many ways, I was finally playing the type of game I wanted.

But losing, particularly that Saints game, really burned me up. While walking off the field, I heard a fan telling Alge Crumpler— my teammate and one of the best tight ends in the league—that he sucked. The guy was wearing a New Orleans Saints jersey; he wasn't one of our fans. But he was with a guy who had on a Falcons jersey. They were together, and both of them started yelling to us, "You guys stink. You guys suck."

It was an odd situation. I was like, *There's a Falcons fan with a New Orleans Saints fan, and both of them are screaming that we suck.* I just felt something wasn't right with that picture.

I became so infuriated that I put my middle fingers up at both of them, as if to say, *You know what? If y'all feel that way, then @#$% y'all.* And I didn't even think anything of it. I just reacted.

Right then, I didn't care. My attitude was, *So what? I stuck my middle fingers up.* I didn't think about who was watching or who was around.

I got a call about an hour later. The team's public relations guy, Reggie Roberts, asked me if I stuck my middle fingers up. My response was, "Nah; well, yeah, I did, but there wasn't anybody out there." He was like, "Man, you lie. There were cameras all over you."

And the next thing you know, that was the hot topic.

I was sternly reprimanded by the team owner, Mr. Blank, and was fined $10,000. I contributed an additional $10,000 to charity—$5,000 to the family of a fallen firefighter and another $5,000 to then-teammate Warrick Dunn's foundation that helps single mothers become homeowners.

I look back and wish I could apologize to those two men and to everyone who witnessed the incident. I wish I had donated even more to charity, and not just money but also my time—because I so deeply regret the incident.

I would never do that now. I had always been a fan-friendly guy at Virginia Tech and in Atlanta. I am embarrassed that I took it there. I was really upset with myself after that because I knew better.

The moment showed my immaturity and was probably a symptom of greater issues in my life. It was the first of many lessons I would soon learn.

I learned that you can't react; you have to respond. I reacted negatively out of emotion; I let my emotions, not the truth, control me. I let those guys get under my skin, and they saw me sweat. They won. For them it was: *Oh, he stuck his middle fingers up at us! We made him mad! He noticed us!*

Instead of letting them win that moment, I should have recognized the truth: Alge and I were Pro Bowl players, excellent at our jobs, and public figures open to criticism. Rather than reacting, I should have simply responded with a "Thanks" and a wave, and then let my play on the field speak for me the following week.

The incident was damaging for me and the Falcons organization, but I think it also demonstrated what kind of emotions players wrestle with during and after a game. We play with a lot of passion. And for all that has ever been said about me, no one can ever say I didn't play with my heart. However, I think if things in my life were different, I would have made a more sound decision in that situation. The incident kind of set everything off. It was as if I hung a black cloud over my head.

Six weeks or so later, at the end of the 2006 season, Coach Mora was dismissed. Little did I or anyone else know at the time, but that season would be my last with the Falcons too—and with the NFL for two long years.

*

Through much of my time in Atlanta, I was dealing with a personal struggle that no one knew about. It was really the only thing that has ever truly affected my concentration on football.

I had dated Tameka steadily for a long time. Six months after I was drafted, we learned that we were pregnant. Just before my second season in Atlanta, Tameka gave birth to our son, my first child, Mitez.

My relationship with Tameka had become strained, and it eventually fell apart. It turned into a custody battle that exhausted me emotionally.

The situation really took a toll on me one season when there was a period of time I didn't know where Mitez and his mother were living. I never wanted to be away from my son, but I found a way to manage. We went back and forth, and I finally got joint custody.

Before that, though, it was a struggle. I was in Atlanta playing football, and I was really frustrated because I was in a situation that money couldn't buy me out of. Like I said, there was half a season when I didn't know where my son was, and that really bothered me. I didn't want to complain to anyone and I didn't want to say anything to anyone, so I kept it all to myself. It was painful.

This is one of the first times I've ever really talked about the situation. It affected more than my time off the field; it carried over to the field of play as well. It hurt. Being a part of Mitez's life was extremely important to me, yet I couldn't talk to Mitez on the phone, couldn't leave him a voicemail, and couldn't find him or his mom. There were days that I went to play a game, and I expected him to be in the stands watching, but he wasn't there. I don't think it changed me as a player or as a leader, because on the outside I was still happy, but on the inside I was hurting.

I realize you can't trap personal struggles inside and allow them to fester; you have to talk about them. It's one of the things I wish I had done differently in Atlanta. I could have reached out to a lot more people for help. I didn't have to struggle alone.

Regardless of what transpired, I appreciated and still appreciate Tameka for what she has done and is doing for Mitez. Tameka and I have an amicable relationship today, and I know Mitez is well taken care of.

Though my life was lived in the spotlight, the situation with my son was not the only thing hidden from public view.

ᵕᶜ

My entire experience in Atlanta could have turned out differently. Regrettably, it can be summed up in two words: *unfulfilled potential.*

The Falcons drafted me expecting more than the two playoff berths (and no Super Bowls). As much as I accomplished, I look back and see that I should have been more committed to my sport.

There is no doubt in my mind that I could have done more. I mean, I was a Pro Bowl quarterback, and I did what was asked of me. I wasn't a slacker, and I did work hard. But there were important things I didn't do.

My life and career began to waver off course in the days, weeks, and months leading up to the 2001 NFL draft. The slippage—hidden from public view—escaped the detection of the league's ultra-thorough background checks. Looking back, I believe if the NFL had known the full truth about what was happening in my life, it's very likely I never would have been the first overall pick in the draft.

Yes, I had issues off the field; and on the field, I relied strictly on my natural physical skills to carry me rather than trying to hone them. The crazy part was that from the time I left school in January 2001 until my Pro Day in March, I did not work out one time. I ate fast food every day—every day! I didn't lift weights, didn't train, didn't run, didn't study any football. I had not thrown a ball since the Gator Bowl game. And yet I ran a 4.33 forty-yard dash at my Pro Day.

It's a marvel that I was sharp and performed so well for the scouts, given my inactivity. I don't know any way to explain it other than the natural ability God gave me kicked in for some reason. I went into my Pro Day like I had been throwing the ball for three months. Still, I can't help but wonder how I would have done if I had prepared and applied myself.

Unfortunately, I continued that trend when I got to Atlanta. Instead of trying to better myself in the game of football, I felt like what I was doing was enough. I mean, I practiced hard and did what the coaches asked me to. I thought my athletic ability was enough.

I look back now and realize I was not taking full advantage of the physical skills God gave me. I should have been spending extra time in the classroom and weight room, but I wasn't. I never devoted any part of Tuesdays—typically our weekly day off—to things such as studying film to prepare for the upcoming opponent or evaluating my past performances. It's something a lot of the best quarterbacks, like Peyton Manning, do. Often, I would go home to Virginia on Tuesdays and put time into things I should have left alone.

Back then I told myself, *Down the road, when I turn twenty-eight or twenty-nine—that's when I'll study the game. That's when I'll get better. That's probably around the time I'll win a Super Bowl anyway. Nobody is expecting me to win it at such a young age right now.*

You know, I was twenty-one, twenty-two, twenty-three, and I

was looking at guys like Chris Chandler, when he was thirty-seven, and Randall Cunningham, who was in his last year with Baltimore. Those guys were older; they knew the game; they understood it; but it took awhile for them to experience success in their careers. Because of that, I thought it just came in time. I hoped it wouldn't take as long for me, but nothing would change my mind about how I was approaching things.

Sadly, I remember all too well how Randall Cunningham and Steve Young extended themselves to me and were willing to help mentor me at the outset of my career, but I quietly and firmly pushed away their assistance and advice.

I had outlets, good outlets. I had people to talk to, but I chose not to take their advice. I chose to do it my way, not necessarily the "right way" like Coach Beamer taught. I never thought I would have to experience the things I went through, nor the adversity I had to face.

The Falcons organization provided me with so much support throughout my time with them. Mr. Blank, the team owner, treated me extremely well. I should have been more willing to build the mentoring relationship—even a father-son kind of relationship—that he wanted to have with me.

He wanted to be a great friend to me: a man of support, and someone I could count on in times of need. I never took advantage of the opportunity to learn from him—a strong leader, a successful businessman, and a man of integrity. I enjoyed him as a person, but I think there were so many more situations where I could have relied on his knowledge and wisdom. I failed to do that, and I think it caused me to venture down dark paths during certain times in my life.

When he extended a helping hand, I walked away from it. I took everything in my life for granted. I felt like I was old enough to make decisions on my own, and I didn't need other people's counsel or advice.

Once I got used to being in the NFL spotlight, I really felt like I had arrived—that I had made it. I became complacent.

It could be said I was a bit like Icarus of Greek mythology. The myth says that he attempted to escape from an island by flying to freedom with wings made of wax and feathers. He was told not to fly too close to the sun or sea; the sun would melt the wax and the sea would add water and weight to the feathers, making the wings useless. He didn't heed the advice, flew too close to the sun, and fell from the sky into the sea.

When you're young—twenty-two or twenty-three years old with the world at your fingertips—you feel like you're a grown man. You feel like you know it all. But as I would later find out, I certainly didn't know it all.

I was flying high in the NFL. But I took shortcuts and built weak, fake wings. I didn't listen to advice, and I too fell from the sky.

7

Part II:

The Fall

Chapter Five

Warning Signs

"The lifestyle I was leading . . . would soon be revealed to the world."

thought 2007 was going to bring great things for me. It was my seventh year in the NFL, it was '07, and my jersey number was 7.

I had built a strong image, which was evidenced by the fact that global corporations such as Nike, Coca-Cola, and AirTran had made large endorsement deals with me.

We had a new coach, Bobby Petrino, who tailored his explosive offense around my abilities. I had learned the system quickly and put myself in position to be successful with it. The system, coupled with my abilities, had Coach Petrino so enthused and encouraged, he told his coaching staff I was going to be the league MVP that year.

Instead, I didn't even make it to the season. My problems began to surface and multiply, all by my own doing.

I can't say I shouldn't have seen my fall coming. It's not as if I just instantaneously plummeted, though that's how it appeared to the public. Mine was a slow, steady fall, with many chances along the way to notice some glaring warning signs that I was headed in the wrong direction—down.

Whether I was too proud or too stubborn to see what was happening, I'm not really sure. What I do know is that I was too selfish to care about what anyone else thought, or even really care about how my actions affected them.

⌒

A lot of my poor decisions and subsequent mistakes can be attributed mostly to two things: my weak resolve in telling people no, and the people I chose to be associated with. I had an entourage of pretty questionable characters—some with their own criminal records—and I was surrounded by them almost all of the time whenever I wasn't playing football.

I acknowledge I was influenced by those around me, but I take full responsibility for my actions and the image they eventually conveyed. Like I said, it was my decision to have that entourage, and it wasn't a good one. It was the first in a series of bad decisions.

My group of friends began to assemble the moment I left Virginia Tech for the NFL. It was some locals from Newport News, their friends, and guys who approached me with something to offer. Even before I took a snap in the NFL, I had the opportunity to lead these men in a different direction. But my immaturity and youth failed us all.

I spent late nights out with the guys at nightclubs, making a myriad of bad choices. Rather than lifting weights and running, I was out drinking and partying. The Falcons had concerns about the people I was hanging around, but I don't believe team officials knew the extent of what I was doing until it was too late. I was a bad leader off the field for those guys. I had become a manipulator and a master illusionist.

The games I was playing were well hidden from the Falcons organization, the NFL, and the public for a long time. And though hidden, my lifestyle and decisions soon caught up to me and began issuing warning signs that I was taking a dangerous path.

A series of embarrassing public and not-so-public incidents began damaging the façade I had built. Some are very well documented. I tell you of these incidents now, not to glorify them or bring up bad memories for others, but to simply clear up false information and reveal the truth. Mainly, the truth about the man I had let myself become—a selfish liar who was too weak to say no to my friends and lead them.

⌒

The warning signs started to appear in 2004.

The first incident is not well known, and truly was a result of an honest mistake made by one of my associates. However, my attitude caused me to be caught in an awkward and embarrassing situation.

It happened while traveling with some of my entourage on a Tuesday—my day off during the season—from Atlanta back home to Virginia. As we passed through the security checkpoint at the airport, a member of my party inadvertently picked up a watch off the X-ray conveyor belt, believing it was mine. He put it in his pocket, we flew home, and he gave it to me. However, it was not my watch; it belonged to an airport screener. He had put his watch through the machine but left it on the belt as he finished something else. After noticing it was missing, the screener contacted his supervisor. They reviewed the surveillance tapes and saw what had happened, saw who it was, and reported it.

A call was made to the Falcons, who then reached out to me. I told them I had the watch, it was an honest mistake, and I would bring it back when I returned to Atlanta on Wednesday. But I didn't return it on my way back; instead, I went straight to practice. This caused several back-and-forth phone conversations between me, the Falcons, and the airport. I eventually gave the watch back six days later, but only after I had caused considerable headaches for everyone involved and frustration for a man who just wanted his watch back.

The situation affected others more than it did me, so I didn't think it was a big deal. And although it all worked out and was minor in the big picture, I should have been paying attention. More importantly, I was not a man of my word.

~~

On my way through Miami International Airport security in January 2007—shortly after the postgame incident in New Orleans (which became known as "dirty birds"), and after our 2006 season ended—I got myself into a precarious situation. TSA authorities confiscated a water bottle from me that had a secret compartment that appeared to have remnants of marijuana.

The incident created quite a stir for the Falcons, who were

extremely upset that their star quarterback was once again making negative news.

Here's what happened: entering the airport that day, I was not in the best frame of mind. As I approached the security checkpoint, I was oblivious to the numerous signs telling passengers they are prohibited from taking liquids or containers through the screening process. Yet I was carrying a water bottle, with what could be viewed as liquid in it, to the checkpoint.

When I approached the screeners, they said, "You can't take that bottle."

I replied, "This is my bottle, and I like it and don't want to throw it away."

They took it, so I said, "Give it to me," and opened it up. "It's not even a water bottle," I remarked as I exposed the compartment to them.

They saw it and responded, "That's even worse. Give it to us." Then they took it and threw it in a recycling bin and let me pass through security.

I boarded my flight and returned to Atlanta. But evidently, because of my odd behavior, they went back and got the bottle from the bin to inspect it. Upon inspection, they thought it smelled funny, and they saw a black substance in the compartment, which led to a police report being filed against me on suspicion of possession of an illegal substance and drug paraphernalia.

When they confiscated the bottle, though, there was nothing in it, and that was proven by the Metro-Dade crime lab. No charges were filed, and the incident was dropped, but only after causing more heartache for the Falcons, the league, and my sponsors.

I was thinking that 2007 was going to be the year of my life—and for that incident to happen three weeks into the year—it was really like a blinking light saying, "Your wings are coming unglued."

The water-bottle incident and the Falcons' publicly stated disapproval still didn't cause me to stop and think about what I was doing.

On April 24, 2007, I skipped a scheduled appearance on Capitol Hill in Washington, DC, at which I was supposed to lobby before Congress for after-school programs. I had spent the previous day participating in Warrick Dunn's charity golf tournament in Tampa, Florida. My AirTran flight from Tampa to Atlanta was delayed, causing me to miss my connecting flight to Washington. Even though there was a later flight to Washington that I could have taken, I inexplicably decided against it. To this day, I really don't know why I didn't take it.

I ended up being a no-show in DC.

Of course, it became a public matter.

I gave my publicist, Susan Bass, incorrect information—blaming the airline—which made her account of the circumstances conflict with the statement AirTran released. I feel bad that, because of me, my publicist looked like she was being untruthful in the press release she issued on my behalf. She believed what I was telling her, so that's what she wrote. She asked me numerous times if it was the truth, and I told her yes. Obviously, it wasn't.

The situation was key to the breakdown in my business relationship with the airline, eventually leading the company—which once had my image adorning its billboards—to end its endorsement contract with me. It had been a sweetheart deal for me; among the perks was that I got to fly for free.

It was very immature of me to blame missing the event in Washington on the airline when it was entirely my fault. Even on my ride home from Atlanta-Hartsfield, my friend Adam Harris said, "You need to get your butt in the car and drive to DC and be there in the morning."

I said, "You know what? It's really not that big of a deal." I talked to him for about fifteen minutes about why I shouldn't go, and finally he just said, "You know what? Forget it."

I should have taken the responsibility and shown everyone that I could be accountable for important meetings and events. It was just another situation where I let my pride get ahead of me. Things that mattered to me once, like helping others and being involved in the community, no longer mattered. I thought I was bigger than it all. I could have been very instrumental in helping out a group of kids. I just didn't want the hassle, nor did I really care at the time. The only person I cared about was me. And though my teammates and those around me didn't really see it, I'd become something I never wanted to be: I had become a "me" guy. Truth is, I just cared about my own time and not much else.

The DC incident was the last warning sign. The lifestyle I was leading, my lies, my entourage, and the illusion I had constructed would soon be revealed to the world.

I changed when I arrived in the NFL. I started to decay.

Chapter Six

Dog Days

"One phone call on April 25, 2007, changed my life forever."

One phone call on April 25, 2007, changed my life forever. I was out playing golf with D. J. Shockley—a backup quarterback for the Falcons—at Sugarloaf Country Club, near my home in the Atlanta suburb of Duluth, Georgia, when my cell phone rang.

My cousin and longtime friend Davon Boddie, who was part of my posse that concerned the Falcons, had been arrested by police five days earlier outside a nightclub in Hampton, Virginia, on charges of possession and distribution of marijuana. He told authorities that his home address was 1915 Moonlight Road in Smithfield, Virginia—a home I owned.

The caller informed me that police had raided the property, discovering evidence of dogfighting and mistreatment of animals, which might potentially lead to felony charges for me and my friends. Suddenly, "dirty birds," water bottles, and missed congressional appearances paled in comparison.

I sensed at the time that this was way bigger than me. In the days that followed, my lawyer asked numerous times if I had any involvement, and I told him no. But I knew I was lying and, at any given moment, it could backfire in my face.

~~

The subject matter I'm about to discuss is highly controversial and sensitive—and understandably so. I want to make it clear from the outset that in no way do I mean to glorify dogfighting or my involvement in it. But I do want to be candid about what happened, and my background with it, to answer any lingering questions that might exist. It needs to be shared because it is part of my story. And I will make it clear that such activity and behavior should be strictly avoided and not tolerated.

~~

I grew up loving animals and had a passion for them. As a boy, I had two parakeets, a few gerbils, and a pet dog named Midnight.

Midnight had a really pretty black coat with brown dots above her eyes. She was a beautiful dog; I fell in love with her. I would go to the local grocery store to help people with their bags, and they'd give me fifteen or twenty cents. At the end of the day, if I could leave with two dollars, I'd have enough to buy two cans of dog food for Midnight. It was like my summer job as a little kid. It let me provide for her.

Midnight was my companion, so I didn't want to do with her what I heard the other guys were doing with their dogs because I was emotionally attached to her.

I saw my first dogfight when I was eight.

One day, a friend and I stepped outside the building where I lived in the Ridley Circle housing project and saw kids and their bicycles surrounding a grassy area where we usually played football. But instead of a football game, about eight pit bull terriers were gathered. Most people don't know this, but back then, just as is the case now, I am scared to death of dogs I don't know. So my friend and I jumped on top of a mailbox to give us spectator seats at a safe distance from what was happening.

We saw guys putting their dogs' faces right in front of one another. The dogs would grab and fight. I remember two of them were fighting when a third, smaller dog jumped on the back of one of the larger dogs to make it two-on-one.

I didn't know what to think of it all. In a way, it captured my attention. But it also seemed mean, even cruel.

The bottom line, however, is that right there, on that very day, my fascination with dogfighting began. It's something I wish had never, ever happened.

I cringe at the brutality of it all now. I didn't realize how wrong dogfighting was at the time. It's the one thing about growing up in the area that I wish I could change. It was just a way of life in the neighborhood. It wasn't out of the norm to walk up and see two guys fighting with their dogs, or to hear a dog in the bushes barking. You knew it was somebody's dog that was being kept to fight. There was no other place to keep them.

It was going on almost every day. Either you would see guys

fighting their dogs against one another, or against dogs belonging to guys from other neighborhoods.

Jamel, my childhood friend, recalls that informal dogfights would happen randomly in the neighborhood. The fascination, he says, would be comparable to lions fighting. It captivates you.

Over the next two years, my friends and I sometimes hid dogs in the bushes around our neighborhood, and we'd let them fight one another.

An older boy, Tony, was one of the first people to teach me about dogfighting. He was about ten years older than me. My friends and I would play basketball with Tony and other older boys. I guess I had impressed them with my athleticism because when I would go to the court, Tony used to pick me to be on his team. He would come to the basketball court with a nice pit bull—always. He was around a lot of the older guys and dope dealers in the neighborhood who had dogs as well.

By the time I was ten, I stopped hanging out with him because I was spending so much time playing sports, fishing, and hanging out at the local Boys & Girls Club. However, I returned to his company nearly a dozen years later and got myself into the first situation that I couldn't lie, manipulate, or buy my way out of.

⌒⌒

I didn't fight dogs again until after I got out of college.

Sometimes when I came home from Virginia Tech, I would run into Tony and talk to him about pit bulls. Tony always told me, "Just let me know when you want a real dog."

I would ask, "What is that supposed to mean?"

One time he said, "Meet me tomorrow at eight o'clock."

So my friend, Quanis Phillips, and I met him, and he took us over to Smithfield, Virginia, to a dogfight. It was the first organized dogfight I had ever seen.

My reaction was, "Man, y'all be doing this?!" The dogs were really fighting; I could tell they were really out to kill each other. I had seen dogfights where dogs snapped at each other, but these dogs actually were locked together, engaged, using strategies to try to hurt one another.

I was looking at it like, *Man, this is crazy.* I hadn't ever seen anything like it—to the point that it scared me. This was nothing compared to what I had seen as a kid.

On one hand, I was intrigued by it. On the other hand, I had never seen anything so furious, so ferocious, and so violent.

⌒

That's the backdrop to the day I made the worst decision of my life: the day when I stopped being a spectator of dogfighting and instead began participating in it with vigor.

It was March 2001, about a month before I was selected by Atlanta in the NFL draft. I was with Quanis at the Esquire Barbershop in Newport News. It was an area of town where there was plenty of trouble. Dope dealers and other questionable characters were usually outside the shop. I turned around and was surprised to see Tony walking past. I said, "Quanis, that's Tony. Let's see if he has some dogs."

By that time I no longer had Midnight; I had a new dog, Champagne, that I had bred. She had some puppies, and I was thinking about selling them, or training and fighting them and getting myself into the lifestyle; but I didn't know how to do it and didn't know where Tony was until that day.

We ran out of the barbershop and I told Tony, "I want some of those dogs like you had last year." He and I arranged to meet the next afternoon and, at that moment, I jumped into the dogfighting world.

I met Tony the next day at two o'clock, and he was in my life every day after that until 2004.

We went and bought two dogs that day, two dogs the next week, and another dog the next week. Tony told me he had a little place to house them. Someone he knew had some land, and we would house them there. They'd be safe.

Tony immediately started giving me lessons, picking up where he'd left off when I was ten. He taught me what to look for in a fighting dog.

He started teaching me the game of schooling and how to find a dog that likes to shoot for the legs—to the point where I got so good at it that I knew more than everyone in the crew. I was good at looking at a dog and knowing its weight, seeing its fighting style, matching up breeding pairs, and getting young dogs that were hot and ready to go. I received intensive training from Tony from April through June of 2001.

As my stable of dogs grew, so did the need to find a new place to house them. I went from having fifteen dogs on some land to buying a piece of property, which was 1915 Moonlight Road in Surry County. I sent Tony on a mission to find that land, and we transported our dogs to our new property. From that point until federal agents shut down the operation six years later, the Moonlight Road location was the home of Bad Newz Kennels.

I built a large house there for many of my friends to live in. I stopped by at least once a week on my Tuesday off-days from the NFL. Behind the house were black buildings where the dogfighting operation was centered—barns, kennels, an infirmary, and an upstairs area where fights took place.

After my imprisonment, I was nauseated by a visit back to the location to shoot a segment for *The Michael Vick Project* documentary, which aired on Black Entertainment Television (BET). But back when I was involved in those activities, I may have become more dedicated to the deep study of dogs than I was to my Falcons playbook. I became better at reading dogs than reading defenses.

That's just so sad to say right now, because I put more time and effort into trying to master that pursuit than my own profession ... which was my livelihood ... which put food on the table for my family. It was that love and that passion for my wrongdoings that led me to lose everything I worked so hard for.

⌒

Over the course of the next six years, Bad Newz Kennels participated in dogfights in various locations in the Carolinas, Virginia,

Maryland, and elsewhere. It was a wild time. I was living life like I was a street guy—we were always around some very rough and intense individuals. I had a separate persona. You never would have known I was a Pro Bowl quarterback.

The fights generally took place in locations far out in the countryside, where there was virtually no population base. We'd conduct them in a desolate area no one knew anything about—where it was hidden and where no one outside the business would know something illegal was going on. However, it seemed like there were usually spectators.

I could go into more detail, but I don't want to teach people how to run a dogfight. I don't want to glorify it. But I will tell you that I know too much about it, and it's something I wish I'd never learned.

⌒

When I was young, I witnessed dogfighting so much that I didn't think it was wrong. But as I grew older, I knew it wasn't right. We would hear about dogfighting operations getting busted. For instance, there was a dogfighting ring that was busted in Chesapeake, Virginia. But I also heard it was mainly a drug-related bust. A lot of guys in the dogfighting game were drug dealers—it was the way they were able to afford their dogs. So, when they were raided for drugs, the authorities found dogs, or vice versa, and either way it seemed like the drug bust routinely made bigger news and received more attention.

So I knew you could get in trouble over dogfighting, but I never heard of anyone being convicted of a felony because of it, or going to jail or being prosecuted. I figured, *It ain't that bad. It's wrong for the dogs, but this is what these dogs like to do. This is why they're bred.* That was my train of thought—that they're bred to fight.

I was so wrong.

My associates and I were so confident we'd never be caught that we ignored some obvious tip-offs. For instance, one of the neighbors near the property on Moonlight Road came over about fifteen days before the raid and told the guys there, "Listen, state police came by and wanted to put a video surveillance camera on my property. They wanted to see all the traffic coming in and out of your house. They want to know what's going on." People were hearing a lot of rumors, but we didn't take that as a sign that we were in trouble.

I was not told about the neighbor's visit until it was too late. The other guys just brushed the neighbor off. If I had known that, I would have shut down the operation. It was too close to home.

This, I think, provides a clear picture of the situation I was in—how I failed to lead the people around me.

⌒

Just a few days before the raid and that phone call, I was out at the property with Quanis and some other guys. What happened out there that day was bad, really bad.

We had gone out and gotten rid of a lot of dogs. It's a day I would like to forget. But I can't. It will always haunt me. It was a day I wasn't even supposed to be there. It was the day I said to myself,

This is it. I'm not dealing with this anymore. I had actually already bought some horses and was getting into show horses. I was ready to move on.

That was the day my conscience began speaking to me about the seriousness of the crimes I was committing. I remember looking at a dog and saying, "I wonder if one day I'll be punished for this." But I said, "You know what? It hasn't happened since we got started in 2001, and look at my life now. Naw, I'm all right."

Everyone in dogfighting was doing the same thing: killing their dogs and getting rid of them when they lost. I had seen guys take the dogs right out of the fighting box and—*bam*—shoot them in the head.

In January 2010, new documents emerged from the dogfighting investigation that my codefendants and I—among other things—allegedly killed dogs with shovels, but that's not true. Nonetheless, I understand that the killings were, and still are, sickening.

Needless to say, I was paralyzed after the phone call I received on the golf course a few days later. I guess I can't say I should have been surprised; I just let my arrogance blind me from the truth of my life, and my ability to lie hid the truth from many around me.

I had kept that world private for six years, which is amazing considering the sophistication of NFL security, where former FBI agents and the like are hired to keep a close watch over the players. But because the dogfighting world is so underground, so low-key, I was able to stay beneath the radar.

The anticipation of taking the field.

Photo by Drew Hallowell/Getty Images

Sharply dressed for my school photo.

Photo courtesy of Michael Vick

The public housing of Ridley Place in Newport News, VA,
where I was born and raised.

Photos by Greg Arnold

Getting my feet wet as a freshman at Ferguson High School.

The No. 7 really fit at Warwick.

Photos by Daily Press

I really grew as a player under Coach Reamon.

On the move for Virginia Tech against Boston College in 2000.

1999 Media Guide photo for the Hokies.

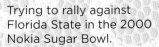

Trying to rally against Florida State in the 2000 Nokia Sugar Bowl.

The crowds in Blacksburg were awesome. Being carried off the field by the fans after our 11-0 season.

Tucking the ball, with an eye downfield against Rutgers in 2000.

Diving over the pile into the endzone. I've always loved flying through the air.

...Shortly after I was picked No. 1 overall by the Atlanta Falcons.

My first NFL regular season game.

Photo by Andy Kuno/AFP

Even the snow couldn't stop us from handing Green Bay its first-ever home playoff loss in 2003.

Photo by Jonathan Daniel/Getty Images

Photo by Drew Hallowell/ Getty Images

With Coach Dungy and Coach Reid at the press conference announcing my signing with the Philadelphia Eagles.

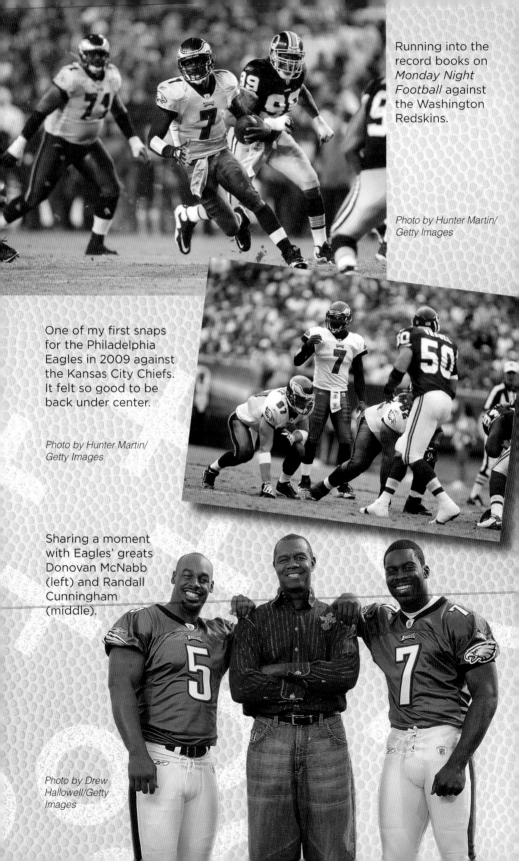

Running into the record books on *Monday Night Football* against the Washington Redskins.

Photo by Hunter Martin/ Getty Images

One of my first snaps for the Philadelphia Eagles in 2009 against the Kansas City Chiefs. It felt so good to be back under center.

Photo by Hunter Martin/ Getty Images

Sharing a moment with Eagles' greats Donovan McNabb (left) and Randall Cunningham (middle).

Photo by Drew Hallowell/Getty Images

Playing in the 2011 Pro Bowl, my first Pro Bowl since 2005.

Photo by Kent Nishimura/ Getty Images

Sharing the stage with my mentor, Coach Dungy, speaking to the inmates in Avon Park, FL.

Talking about the true freedom of
the gospel with an inmate during
my visit to the prison.

Photo by Chris Shigas

(L-R) Wayne Pacelle, President of the Humane Society of the United States; Michael Vick; and Chris Shigas, Vice President at French/West/Vaughan, prepare to enter the United States Capitol, where we appeared before Congress to support legislation strengthening animal welfare laws.

Speaking at the Camelot Schools graduation in 2011.

Photo by Gilbert Carrasquillo/Getty Images

After the raid of the house on Moonlight Road where dogfighting evidence was found, I said publicly, "I'm never at the house," when in reality I went there regularly, including most Tuesdays during the football season. Three days after police raided my house in Smithfield, I met with NFL commissioner Roger Goodell. I assured him of my innocence and was permitted to participate in a ceremony at the April 28, 2007, NFL draft with other former Virginia Tech players Bruce Smith and DeAngelo Hall, to memorialize students who had recently been killed in a shooting spree on the Blacksburg campus.

I really like Commissioner Goodell. He's a very humble, fair, firm, and stern man who cares about you. He wants to see the right things for the integrity of the NFL and the integrity of the football family. If you cross the guidelines of the conduct policy, he wants to know what the absolute truth is.

I knew how to lie with a straight face. Sad to say, Commissioner Goodell bought into what I was saying, and I think he truly believed me that I was telling the truth. I deeply regret not telling him the truth from the outset.

It was a very nervous time for me. I knew I was going to try to lie my way through the whole dogfighting case and see if money, good lawyers, and manipulating the system could get me out of the position I was in—which was a terrible position. Temporarily, I received a reprieve from the commissioner, but it would be short-lived.

Falcons owner Arthur Blank, and my coach at the time, Bobby Petrino, also believed me and trusted in me. If you had told Mr.

Blank I was fighting dogs, he probably would've told you to get out of his face. He trusted me. So did a lot of people who had no idea I was living a lie.

Commissioner Goodell, Mr. Blank, and Coach Petrino were the three key components to my future and my career. They all had trust in me.

Looking back, I can see that my propensity for trying to lie my way out of trouble only made my consequences more severe. I got used to not being honest in a lot of situations. I got away with it for so long that I started to get into a routine and feel like, *Hey, if it worked last time, it will work again.*

I've figured out since then that if you just tell the truth, it's so much easier to deal with the consequences in the beginning than if you lie and someone else reveals the truth. When that happens, people look at you like, *I can't trust him. He's not honest. He's not loyal. He's not forthright, and I can't believe him moving forward.* It screws up everything. Just deal with the consequences. Be a man and deal with it.

Telling the truth is freeing. I found that when I lied, I put pressure on myself. Maintaining the lie was hard work because I had to pile one new lie on top of another. The truth is the truth, and that's it. In the long run, you will benefit from telling the truth even if it comes with consequences.

～

As the investigation deepened, my lawyer told me, "If you were involved, you need to tell me you were involved." That's when it was on the state, rather than the federal, level. I kept telling him, "No, no, I wasn't involved, no." The whole time investigators were building the case, my lawyer was saying no, but he was seeing all this evidence saying yes. If I had just told the truth, maybe I would have received a smack on the wrist instead of a lengthy sentence.

If there had never been an indictment, I might have gotten out unscathed, and the full truth might never have been revealed. But when all the lies were exposed, it was tough. When the Feds got involved, they found all the evidence they needed. They had all the components to basically put me in jail, even without me saying anything.

When they indicted me, we all knew I was wrong. Fittingly, the nation was outraged by my dogfighting activities, which I eventually described as "barbaric." Lots of people wanted to see me severely punished.

In June 2007, a federal grand jury charged me and my three codefendants—Tony Taylor, Quanis Phillips, and Purnell Peace—with conspiring to operate a dogfighting business and doing so across state lines, while also procuring and training dogs to participate in the operation. All four of us originally pled not guilty, but Tony, Quanis, and Purnell eventually changed their pleas and agreed to participate in the case against me. I was implicated not only in dogfighting, but also in helping to kill dogs and bankrolling the gambling part of the operation. Tony, Quanis, and Purnell gave detailed descriptions of my involvement in the Bad Newz Kennels dogfighting operation in which they too were participants.

The evidence was so thorough, so convincing, that I decided to forgo a trial. On August 23, 2007, I signed a plea agreement and, four days later, pled guilty to a dogfighting conspiracy before US District Judge Henry Hudson in Richmond, Virginia, filing a confessional statement of facts that led to my imprisonment and sentencing. I held a press conference afterward, apologizing and vowing to redeem myself.

I truly was sorry for my actions, as my confidant and pastor of Psalms Ministry, Domeka Kelley, knew perhaps better than anyone. He was probably the first person I sat down with and confessed to about all I had done—before I pled guilty or said anything publicly admitting my fault. He could tell that it was difficult for me to talk about—that I was sincere—and he prayed with me.

After my troubles became public, my first coach in Atlanta, Dan Reeves, said that he never had any reason to think I was involved with dogfighting. "I was surprised, because Mike had a dog he would bring to practice," Coach Reeves told the public. "He loved his dog. Personally, I didn't think that was something he would do because he was a dog lover. . . . But he certainly made a huge mistake."

As would be expected, I was bombarded with negative publicity as soon as the news broke about the dogfighting. However, I didn't expect what I perceived to be a public attack by my father. In interviews with the *Atlanta Journal-Constitution* and the *Washington Post* in late August 2007, my father said he warned me to stop dogfighting and that he believed I got involved in the practice during my college days at Virginia Tech. He also said I used to have dogfights in the garage of our family's Newport News home.

He acknowledged that I had recently turned down his request for money, around $700,000. But what about the fact that he was living in an apartment that I was paying for at that time?

I felt betrayed. I felt like my very own father had thrown me under the bus. What made matters worse is that his information was false. This did great damage to our relationship. We had arguments so severe that we were ready to fistfight.

If anything, those articles with my dad were supposed to be positive, and he was supposed to be very supportive, letting the world know I made a mistake and accepted responsibility for my wrongdoings. But for him to make matters worse was very, very disappointing to my family and mind-boggling to me.

It is absolutely false that I had any involvement in dogfighting while at Virginia Tech. And even though my father attended some of my games there, he certainly wasn't aware of what I did on campus.

I felt like everything I had worked for in developing a relationship with my dad and helping him was practically undone at the time. I wanted no more part of him. I forgave him when he did it, but I knew it would be awhile before I could talk to him and honestly confront him about the situation.

Basically, what my dad did hurt my case. From that point on, I made a vow to myself: I was going to try and do the right things in my life moving forward; I wasn't going to let the outside world have an effect on me; I was going to be conscious of the people I let into my life, even if it was family.

I believe my dad was jealous of the role my high school coach, Tommy Reamon, played in my life as I grew up and developed into an NFL quarterback. It wasn't only jealousy, though, that I believe motivated my father's comments, which seemed bizarre to me. He was doing drugs at that time, and I saw the effect it had on the person I thought I knew.

I took that with me to prison too. Until he changed his life, he was a scary person to be around. But the thing is, he's usually a very giving, likable person. When he did what he did, you could see how drugs could change a person.

Thankfully, my relationship with my father began to mend after I was released from prison, and it has improved steadily since then. He's gotten his life into a much better place too.

⌒

My legal troubles led the Falcons to pursue a return of some of the signing-bonus money they had already paid me for my contract from 2004. The club initially aimed to get back $20 million, but eventually was awarded the right to about $6.25 million.

I'll be honest: when Mr. Blank came after the signing-bonus money, I kind of had mixed feelings about it. Together, we changed the culture and the whole perspective on Atlanta Falcons football. I felt like I had helped that franchise generate a lot of money. When he asked for the signing bonus back, the only thing I could think was, *Why would he do that if he cared so much about me and my family and what I did to help the Falcons organization?*

But on the flip side, I think about how he sat me in his office, asked me to be honest—told me to just tell the truth about every-thing—and I didn't. I also realized how much trouble my dif-ficulties caused for Mr. Blank and the Falcons. Everything from imaging to business and financial affairs was affected. So, hon-estly, at the end of the day, no, I wasn't upset. I understood. I'm a guy who believes if you're right, you're right, and if you're wrong, you're wrong. I was totally wrong. So I can't be mad at Mr. Blank for doing what he thought was right.

Since those difficult days, I'm humbled to say that Mr. Blank hasn't turned his back on me; we continue to have a strong rela-tionship. After my life and career got turned around, he contacted me multiple times during the 2010 season to communicate words of encouragement.

It's nice to have a friend you can count on—who will be there caring for you throughout life no matter what mistakes you've made.

After all I did to hurt his franchise, he could've chosen to dis-tance himself rather than to draw close, but he is that kind of person—a good person—for what he does as a philanthropist, for what he does in the community, for what he does for his football team and his players. He truly cares.

He'll forever receive blessings. It's why the Lord sent Matt Ryan to be his new quarterback and Mike Smith to be their coach. Both of them are excellent at what they do, and that's why they're having success. Wide receiver Roddy White has emerged as a great player. They've got a great running back in Michael Turner, they signed pass rusher John Abraham on defense, and they're filling up the stands. Mr. Blank is going to reap his blessings.

I screwed up down there in Atlanta. I feel bad about it, and I wish I could redo it all. But we can't go back. Mr. Blank is enjoying his life. He's enjoying football. I'm doing the same. It's what we both desired for each other. I never wanted to see that franchise fail, and I never once rooted against them. I want to see them excel, and they've been doing that.

Not only did I hear from the Falcons as my legal troubles mounted, I heard from the league too.

I heard from Commissioner Goodell only in the form of a stern letter. He didn't call to ask why I lied or why I didn't tell the truth. He didn't have to—it was all in the indictment. He knew I was a liar. I felt so bad. There was no one to turn to and no one to explain anything to, because I had done all the explaining I could do at the time. It was all a lie anyway—trying to protect myself, my endorsements, everything I worked for, and what little credibility I had left.

Before going to prison, I failed a drug test during my third week on probation for smoking marijuana. Then the only thing Commissioner Goodell did was send someone from the NFL substance abuse program—a policy guy—out to the house to drug test me twice a week during the month before I was incarcerated. It was all I ever heard from Commissioner Goodell. I didn't meet with the commissioner again until after I was released from prison. We didn't talk; there was just silence. Later on, he did pass a couple of messages through my agent, just to see how I was doing, to see if I was okay. But I didn't expect to hear from him. I had lied to him. Whatever trust he had in me, I threw it down the drain.

⌒

Looking back, I'm deeply sorry for everything that happened and how it happened. I wish I could turn back the hands of time and do it differently. I understand that what I did was wrong. I especially wish I'd never talked to Tony that day in March 2001. But it was a choice I made. It was my fault.

If I had the chance to take back one thing that I have done in my life, it would be what happened to those dogs. But I got caught up in that lifestyle and my own lies, and I didn't change or see that I needed to change at the appropriate time. The only thing I can do now is to try to make it right by seeking to help more animals than I have hurt by doing things like speaking to kids, schools, and groups through the Humane Society about the evils of dogfighting.

⌒

Now, when I reflect on everything, I believe God intervened when He needed to in order to put a stop to it. He had been giving me all those warning signs; He was gently trying to get my attention. Unfortunately for me, though my wings were coming unglued, it wasn't enough. So He had to hit me with something harder.

He gave me a chance. He gave me three months—April through July—to go to all these people and say, "Look, I was wrong." He gave me the opportunity to get the correct advice and use it. But I didn't do it.

Eventually, it was as if God said, "Kid, I offered you a chance to get this thing right. Now carry yourself to jail." I know He didn't say it like that, but I can imagine Him saying, "Go on. You need to do some time. You need to learn a lesson."

Chapter Seven

Family Matters

"I hit the ground hard. I was leaving my foundation—my family."

had become a "me" guy. Nothing else mattered.

But during the weeks leading up to November 19, 2007—the day I began serving my prison sentence—I realized how valuable my family was. Not to say they weren't important before, but I had certainly become preoccupied and distracted with things I shouldn't be involved in, things that took me away from my family.

I was flying high—blinded by the clouds—unable to see my foundation below. But in the weeks leading up to November 19, I could see it better than ever.

I hit the ground hard. I was leaving my foundation—my family.

⌒

I wasn't planning on going out that night. But I'm glad I did.

It was 2002, and my friends were trying to get me to go to a nightclub one night in Virginia.

"C'mon," they told me. "C'mon, let's go hang out."

All I wanted to do was relax. It was the offseason. And I didn't feel like going anywhere. But I went.

The nightclub is where I met the woman who would become my wife, Kijafa. I wouldn't call it "love at first sight," but it was pretty close. I'd call it more of an "apple of my eye" experience. I was looking at her across the way. She had a round face, pretty eyes, and a certain demeanor about her. She was cute, and for some reason, she stood out to me.

I asked her to come over.

She didn't—just like a girl is supposed to do.

I laugh about it now and will tell my daughters to do the exact same thing Kijafa did. A man is supposed to approach the girl.

We did, however, exchange numbers. But I ended up losing it that week and had to get it again from one of her friends.

It was about 8:00 p.m. one evening, and I was in a Walmart shopping with my friends when I decided to give her a call. But I didn't expect to talk to Kijafa for as long as I did.

I dialed the number. A Chinese woman picked up the phone.

"You've reached such-and-such cuisine," the Chinese voice said. "What would you like to order?"

"Who is this?" I asked, confused.

"Such-and-such cuisine," she said again.

"Oh, well, I've got the wrong number. Sorry."

"I'm just playing," the woman laughed. "It's Kijafa."

Right then and there, I learned a little about her personality. She was outgoing. She wasn't timid or shy like some women. She was charismatic and had a lot to talk about.

We talked for an hour and a half that night, and it felt like I had known her for years. I can't explain it. She really didn't know that I was a football player. Her friends told her who I was at the club, which probably made her even more hesitant to come talk to me because of the negative perception of some football players. But because she didn't know anything about football, she really had no idea that I was the quarterback for the Atlanta Falcons.

I remember her coming to a game one time. I would periodically look up at her in the stands, and she was usually looking down at her phone, playing a game. She didn't understand football. And she didn't know what I did. But she still respected my job and was okay with who I was.

She asked a lot of questions about the game once we started dating. I've kind of been her quarterback coach the last five years. Now she can tell you all about downs and yardages. She even tweets about the game while I'm playing. Teaching her about cover 2—well, that's a different story. I think she even likes being my nurse when I get hurt, because she treats me as if I'm about to leave this earth or something. She caters to me and spoils me. It's awesome.

When I hung up the phone that night, Quanis looked at me in shock. "Who was that you were on the phone with?!?" he asked.

"Kijafa. That was my first time talking to her," I said.

"Boy, you were on the phone for an hour and a half."

I have no idea what happened in that Walmart.

From that point on, I talked to Kijafa every day on the phone. I called her four to five times a day while she was working in a shoe department, and she always picked up the phone and talked to me. More than anything, it was a friendship. I made her laugh. And she made me laugh.

As this continued, I remember Quanis looking at me one day. "You really like that girl," he said.

"Yeah, I think I do," I replied.

The first time Kijafa and I hung out face-to-face was at my house. We talked all night, and I took her on a four-wheeler ride at four in the morning. She loved it.

In 2009—after all we'd been through together—I proposed to her on her twenty-ninth birthday. I planned a surprise party and told her that we were going out to eat at the Ritz-Carlton. When we got there, I asked the lady up front about a party downstairs, and I told Kijafa one of my teammates was attending the party. We went downstairs to "see my teammate." When we opened the doors, everyone yelled "Surprise!" Several friends and family members were there who she hadn't seen in a while. That was a surprise in itself.

Little did she know.

A slow song came on, and I asked her to dance with me. I was thinking about what I was going to say, and I started sweating. Not only was I going to ask her to marry me, but I was also doing it on national television for the *Michael Vick Project* by BET.

"Baby, wipe the sweat off my head," I said.

She did.

"I'm so nervous," I told her. "I'm so nervous."

"Why?" she laughed.

Then I stopped dancing.

"You don't want to dance with me," she said.

I was just standing there, looking stupid. Then I got down on one knee. After all I put her through—seven years of dating, eighteen months in prison, the times I should have listened to her and I didn't, the times I should have been more respectful and I wasn't—I felt like I owed it to her.

We married on June 30, 2012. There are certain people in your life you never want to part ways with. And she's the one I never want to part ways with—not just because of our two daughters, but because of the friendship we've developed over the years and our ability to love one another and respect one another.

We had been through a lot together. Our relationship continued to develop—from the first call at Walmart to the proposal. We grew closer along the way, and even closer when I went to prison.

When I went to prison, I already had all three of my children. It's what made things even more difficult.

My first child and only son, Mitez, was five years old when I left. He lives with his mother, Tameka Taylor, but he still visits me often.

I missed his birth—who knows what I was doing? But I'll forever remember arriving at the hospital, looking at Mitez, and noticing his cone-shaped head. For the first hour I was there, I was going back and forth with the nurse about the shape of his head. It's funny to look back at it now. The nurse told me that if I kept rubbing it, his head would eventually round out, so that's all I did for the next couple of days.

Still, it was special holding him that first time. I just remember thinking, *This is my child. This is my son.* It was surreal.

From that point on, I knew I had more responsibility. I was a father.

I want to be an example for Mitez, and I want him to learn from my mistakes. I want him to take on something other than football. However, if he plays football, I'll support him, but I don't want him to play just because of me. Maybe he'll be a great artist, musician, lawyer, chief of police—I don't know—but I want him to grow up and change someone's life. I want him to have his own identity. There's only one me and only one him. His destiny is his destiny.

Looking back on raising Mitez in those early years, I think I'll remember the way we used to wrestle. He was relentless. The only way he'd go to sleep was if he wrestled his way to sleep. I was his punching bag.

Along with wrestling, he also likes to golf. He already plays with a set of Callaway clubs that I bought him, and he is pretty good. More importantly though, Mitez is on the A-B honor roll at school. He is a great student. He also challenges his mind; he loves to play chess and is adept at math.

It is different with Mitez than with the girls. He was around earlier in my career and has seen more. He figured out quickly that his dad is sort of well known—whether it's people asking for my autograph or wanting a photograph taken with me.

Once, I was afforded a teaching moment with Mitez because of the attention that often comes my way. We were at a mall, and a store owner shut down his business so we could shop without people bothering us. It gave us alone time, but it was obvious to Mitez that things were different. He saw all of that and said, "Dad, can we have a day where it's just me and you and no one else? No autographs, no pictures?"

I told him, "Son, I wish we could, but that's just not the way it's going to be. We need to be polite. If we didn't want to go out, we could have stayed around the house. So, if you're ever in this situation, I want you to do the same things Daddy does."

Another memory I have of him isn't as pleasant as the wrestling, the golf, or our teaching moment at the mall.

When I went to prison, I didn't have to explain it to my two daughters. Jada was two years old, and London was only a month old. They were too young. Mitez, however, was five.

I'll never forget it. We were watching television together, and a clip of me playing football came up on the screen. Then it came across the news that "Michael Vick could be sentenced to several years in prison." Mitez immediately burst out crying—uncontrollably.

"I don't want you to go to jail!" he screamed.

I was hurt. I was ashamed. And it was all my fault.

How disappointing is that for your son to be watching you on TV and they show a highlight of you in an NFL uniform—which he's accustomed to seeing—and in the next breath, they're talking about you going to prison? That's folly. That's confusion. I didn't know what to tell him other than to be honest. I told him why I was going to jail. And all I could do was pray everything would turn out right.

⌣

Kijafa and I took the next step in our relationship when Jada, our first child and my first daughter, was born.

It was a new lifestyle for me. Instead of living with my friends in Smithfield, I moved in with Kijafa to help her raise Jada. Before that, she would come and stay with me. But living with her was when I got to know Kijafa on a different level. Having a newborn baby to care for made our bond even stronger. I had a family for the first time, and I liked it.

I've always wanted to have a girl, and I took a liking to my new lifestyle. It wasn't as hard as I thought it would be or as bad as people said it would be. I enjoyed every moment of it. I was with my girlfriend—who I loved dearly and would eventually marry— and my daughter, who I needed to support and protect.

Because I was in the house, Jada became just like me. If she was a boy, there's no doubt in my mind that she would be the next Michael Vick on the football field. She has all the athleticism in the world. Strong willed. Fearless. At seven years old, she's sixty pounds of all muscle.

Whenever I got home and walked through the front door, Jada would follow me up the stairs and all around the house. She still does the exact same thing.

Kijafa said that when I went to prison, Jada, for the first six months, would ask, "When is my daddy coming home? Where's my daddy at?"

One day she came home from school, looked all around the house, searched all the rooms, and cried, "Mommy, I've lost my daddy. I can't find him."

Again, all because of me. Your sin doesn't just hurt you: it hurts others.

But I'll forever cherish that phase of my life when I got to be in the house with Kijafa and care for a newborn baby. I didn't have that opportunity with Mitez because Tameka and I were no longer together. And I didn't know it at the time, but I wouldn't have that opportunity with London either, because of my prison sentence.

Being with my family was something I chose to do. Continuing to live with my friends may have sounded more appealing at the time because it's what I was used to. But I remember saying to myself, *It's starting here . . . right now . . . at the age of twenty-four. I'm doing the right thing. This is what a real man is supposed to do.*

Life was exciting. We were living in a brand-new house, we had a new baby, and we had a new way of living.

Everything just felt right . . . for once.

⌒

It's only fitting that I introduce my youngest daughter, London, through my grandmother Caletha . . .

Every night, my grandmother watched the news. She saw my game highlights all the time, and she was in awe that I was her grandson. "I can't believe you made it pro," she'd always tell me. "I can't believe you made it pro."

Even as a professional football player on a rigorous schedule, I continued to regularly drop by her house. That's how important she was to me.

"Are you eating enough?" she'd ask me as I walked in the door. "You big enough? I can't believe you made it pro."

When London was born one month before I went to prison, I knew she was going to be different. Her head, ears, and complexion were all different. She just had a different aura about her. As she grew older, I realized that she actually looked *exactly* like my grandmother.

It hurt that I wouldn't be there with her like Kijafa and I had raised Jada. I wouldn't be in the house. We wouldn't be caring for a newborn baby together. Instead, I'd be in a jail cell.

As the news and negativity unfolded, I avoided my grandmother. She had developed Alzheimer's, but she continued to watch the news—every night—and I figured she knew something was up.

My last stop before I turned myself in was my grandmother's house.

"Where are you going?" she kept asking me.

I couldn't bring myself to tell her the truth. It would hurt her too much.

"Training camp," I lied.

Camp was in the summer—when it was hot. This was November. She knew something wasn't right.

"Where are you going?"

"Training camp."

My mother didn't tell me until a year ago, but my grandmother ended up calling my mom after I left.

"You better tell me the truth," my grandmother said. "Is he really going to training camp?"

Mom said she couldn't help but tell her the truth.

Then my grandmother cried like never before.

"I can't believe this," she cried. "I can't believe he's going to jail."

My grandmother's oldest son basically spent his entire life in prison. She became used to it; she knew that was his life. But she never wanted that for any of us. And for *me*? After all my work to get where I was?

She couldn't believe it.

Chapter Eight

The Prison Experience

"At that moment, my freedom was gone."

There was no more waiting for the worst. It had arrived.

I woke up on November 19, 2007, to a cloudy, gloomy day, which matched the way I felt inside. It was the day I had been dreading for weeks. It was time to leave my family to go to jail and begin serving a prison term that was still three weeks from being finalized in my sentencing hearing.

Turning myself in early was one way of putting myself at the mercy of the court. I hadn't helped my case two months earlier when I'd failed a drug test while on supervised release.

The day I had to leave my family behind was one of the saddest days of my life. My family and I rode from our home in Hampton, Virginia, to the courthouse in Richmond, and from there I was taken to jail in Warsaw, Virginia.

The time leading up to that point meant a lot to me. Every day counted—every hour, every minute, every second—even at night, going to sleep.

I woke up that morning and I told myself, *This is the day*.

Jada could tell something was different about that day.

When I walked into the bathroom to brush my teeth, she asked Kijafa, "Mommy, what are we doing?" She said it with a crack in her voice, as if she sensed that something wasn't right, as if she was wondering, *Why are we getting up so early? Where are we going?*

When I walked back into the room, Kijafa was lying on the bed crying because she knew it was real. We cried on the bed and finally got ourselves together. Kijafa later told me that she was so distraught, she felt her life was almost over.

My security guard, Paul Wilmeyer, drove us to the Richmond Courthouse. Off and on while we were in the car, I just kept crying. I'd cry and I'd cheer myself up, then cry some more and cheer myself up. Even in the car, every minute counted. We were forty-five miles away, so we had just under an hour to get composed and enjoy what little time we had left. Then we were thirty miles . . . twenty miles . . . ten miles away . . .

"Babe, let's go back," Kijafa would say over and over. "Let's run away."

When we pulled up to the courthouse, Kijafa looked me dead in the eyes. "Don't go," she said. "Don't leave."

Then she started crying.

Then Jada started crying—outraged—like there was a monster trying to get her.

Then I started crying.

The pain they felt—it was all my fault.

I had no more fight in me. I was done. Forced to walk away from the car, I shook hands with Paul and shook hands with my close friend CJ Reamon. Then I told everyone that I loved them, and I walked up to the two officers who were waiting for me. When I walked myself in, they started cuffing my hands and legs right there on the spot.

At that moment, my freedom was gone.

⌒

I was led to a car for a ninety-minute drive to Warsaw, Virginia, where I would be incarcerated at Northern Neck Regional Jail for the first two months of my term. I thought I was going directly to the penitentiary camp, but when we arrived at Northern Neck, I wondered, *Why am I coming here?* I thought everyone had it all set up so I would go straight to the camp; I didn't know that I had to stay at the regional jail until I was transferred.

As I was getting checked in, they gave me a black-and-white jumpsuit. It was unlike anything I've ever felt before. I thought to myself, *Man, I guess I'm going to be staying here for a while.*

They took me to my cell—a one-man cell—and they closed the door. It was right in front of booking—right in front of everything. I looked around, overcome by the feeling. *So this is where I'm going to be living?* I thought to myself. *This is where I have to stay? Two hours ago, I was with my family, free. Now I'm in prison, doors slammed.*

I was a caged bird.

⌒

I would hear that sound many times—a prison door slamming shut. It was loud—metal on metal—and there was something harsh and final about it. Especially that first time.

Already, I wanted out. I wanted to escape. I started feeling claustrophobic. The cell room had a metal sink, a metal toilet, a stand-up shower, and a blue metal bunk bed. The cinder-block walls were white and tan. There was a bright white light in the room that I couldn't turn on or off. They turned it off automatically at 11:00 p.m.—"lights out" time. I had a TV and a phone.

I immediately tried to call my mom because I was going into a state of panic. It was a completely disastrous feeling. But the phone wasn't working. So I tried to distract myself by preparing my bunk bed. I got up in the bunk, and I'll never forget it—I just lay in the bed, with my hands over my eyes, and tried to go to sleep. I was in disbelief. *This can't be*, I told myself over and over. I tried to take a nap, but I couldn't. Next, I stood up and put the TV on. There wasn't a clock in the room, so I didn't know what time it was. It just so happened, though, that through the crack of my door, I could look out through booking and see a clock so I could keep track of the time.

It felt like an eternity.

Eventually, it was 7:30, and the guards brought me a tray of food. The food looked awful. I was thinking, *This is what I have to eat?*

From riches to rags. From the NFL to a jail cell.

It was only day one, and I felt like I had been there for eight days. I'll never forget watching *Dancing with the Stars* and just wishing,

Man, if only I had my freedom. I'd do anything for my freedom right now.

People kept coming to the door, checking on me. Every time that door opened, I was hopeful it was going to be a guard saying, "So-and-so called and said to set you free." I was optimistic someone was coming to get me and bail me out, but it never happened.

The first day felt like the longest day of my life, and the second day was even longer. I didn't sleep well. I woke up continually, hoping it was all just a nightmare, but there I was, still in prison.

The first morning you wake up, you don't know when you're coming home. You don't know what your loved ones are doing. I couldn't see a light at the end of the tunnel because there wasn't an end. All I could see was darkness. I was just in prison, knowing I had a court date, knowing I was going to get sentenced, and yet not knowing when I was going home.

I missed my family. It was lonely not being beside Kijafa—not being with Jada, not being with my newborn baby. I missed lying down with all of them. I cried myself to sleep every night.

I've never been so sad, so dismayed. The next day, my phone was working and I called home to my mom. I called every day, crying—called Kijafa crying, just worrying about what she was doing. It took me a couple of weeks to get strong, to strengthen up and say, "Okay, you know what? I have to do this, and I have to get through it."

⌒

When the day for my sentencing hearing finally arrived—December 10, 2007—I woke up early, around 4:00 a.m. I felt optimistic, hoping that I'd only have to spend six to eight months total in prison.

At the time, I was still in that small one-man cell in Northern Neck Regional Jail in Warsaw. I knelt on the side of the bed, and I prayed that everything would be okay—that the sentence would be light.

The prison officials drove me approximately ninety minutes from Warsaw to Richmond for the hearing before Judge Henry Hudson. My family and friends met me there. We were all stunned when Judge Hudson announced a twenty-three-month sentence.

Twenty-three months?! I thought to myself.

It was like my whole world came crashing down. I didn't expect a sentence that long. Everyone was in tears; everyone was distraught. We wanted explanations. We wanted to know why.

When Judge Hudson announced my term, Kijafa kept waiting for him to clarify it. She expected him to maybe say "twenty-three months *of probation*" or "twenty-three months *of home confinement.*" But not this.

She was sad that Jada wouldn't see me for nearly two years—sad that London wouldn't even know who her father was. Because Kijafa didn't grow up with a father figure in her life, she wanted her kids to have a positive father figure in their lives. And here I was, sentenced to twenty-three months in jail.

Once I returned to my cell in Warsaw, I fell onto my bed and cried for about an hour. That's when I hit rock bottom. That's when I hit the ground—when I crashed.

All I could think was, *For the next twenty-three months, I will be incarcerated.* I couldn't take care of my family; I couldn't do anything for my family.

I remember it vividly. I cried; then I stopped. Then I stood up and said, "Okay, I'm ready to go. Let's do it."

⌒

Letters of encouragement or communication of any kind helped me early on.

I remember the first letter from my mother. The first thing I noticed was that she had horrible handwriting! But she really opened up. It's one thing I began to realize—that people can sometimes express more in writing than they can face-to-face. It may be easier to write things than to say them out loud.

What she wrote about were things I wasn't even thinking about. She was just very encouraging, very uplifting, and told me how she was looking forward to my last day.

Over time, I received personal visits from former Atlanta teammates Alge Crumpler, Keion Carpenter, and Kynan Forney; plus Curtis Martin, one of the best running backs in NFL history. It all helped me to know people cared, especially since it wasn't easy for them to get on the prison lists to visit me.

When people came, we talked about everything—what was going on in the outside world and what the new music was, for example. We talked about working out and about all the experiences we had in Atlanta. We talked about relationships. We talked about moving forward and about how I could become a better man—a better person.

I received letters once a week from someone on the Virginia Tech coaching staff. Whether it was head coach Frank Beamer, assistant coach Bryan Stinespring, the defensive coordinator, or the head of football operations, someone wrote me a letter. They stayed in touch. It helped keep my spirits high.

Oddly, I was able to feel the family atmosphere of Tech again, and I knew they cared as much about me as I cared about them.

＜＜

Slowly, painfully, I began to adapt to life in prison.

There was nothing like having my freedom taken away from me—being told when to eat, when to sleep, when to get up, or when I could go outside on the track. I was a twenty-seven- or twenty-eight-year-old *man*, and I was taking orders . . . from another man. It was just a miserable feeling that I had to learn to tolerate and accept.

I was around 500 men every day, in a place I didn't want to be. It was rough. I had to learn how to live the prison life—how to move in prison, how to talk; and I learned when to say something, when not to say something, what to say and what not to say.

In prison you can't show your emotions around others because, in the end, it only puts you at risk for resentment or abuse from other inmates. You just have to be strong, and you have to be able to overcome all the elements in the prison system. It can be brutal; and if you're not strong mentally, you'll break down. Then everyone will see you break down, and you'll have guys taking advantage of you and stealing your commissary purchases. I saw it happen to other guys.

One incident when I had to keep my emotions in check was during a basketball game. Another inmate, who wasn't happy with how things were going for his team, started a fistfight with me. He said, "Because you have money, you can do certain things. I don't care. @#$% you, @#$% you, @#$% you." He cursed at me three times, and I felt I was being disrespected. The next thing I knew, we were in an altercation. It didn't go as far as both of us wanted it to go, and it was probably good that it didn't, but I was to the point that I didn't care at the time. He ticked me off.

You can't be disrespected in front of your peers in prison because a lot of them will look at you like you can be taken advantage of. Experiences like that forced me to adapt quickly, whether I wanted to or not.

The only reason I think I was able to adapt was because of the way I grew up—my upbringing, the environment I was in, the people I was around, and the way God made me. Prison helped mold and shape me as a man. I had to have that experience in order to move forward and become the type of man I've always wanted to be.

I was no longer No. 7, the football player. I was inmate No. 33765-183, and I couldn't change that, regardless of the fact that this number definitely didn't fit me.

I had that number on every day. I had to write it on each piece of mail that I sent out. It will forever be embedded in my brain.

It was stressful. I wanted to break out, wanted to get out, but I couldn't. I was in the same place with the same people every day, all day, with the same guards telling me what to do, what I could or couldn't do, and sometimes, just for spite, conducting shakedowns. It was a constant mess.

There were times I was down and out and just feeling like I was the scum of the earth. But there was another side telling me I could pick myself up and make this all right. Adapting to the environment didn't just mean properly handling conflicts. It also meant trying to stay uplifted, which is probably one of the most important and yet most difficult things to do in there.

When you're in prison, it makes you feel like there is no hope. I was very discouraged at times. But at the same time, I held my head up high, and I knew what was most important. There was the fact that I didn't have to spend my entire life there. One day, I was going to go home and have another chance, a chance to make amends and make things right. It was the only thing I was focused on after a while.

I never lost hope because I had so many of my fans and so many people who wrote me every day. It was like I was talking to them. They wrote back so frequently that I was able to know what was going on in the outside world. It helped me keep my mind. I felt loved by family members, people I had never met, coaches, and others.

I received about 27,000 letters, and only six or seven were hate mail. I read all of them. And I responded to most of them. People were thinking about me when they didn't have to be thinking about me. I was humbled.

Writing letters helped pass the time. I watched television, worked out, wrote letters, made a quick phone call, and before I knew it, I had burnt five hours. So then I'd do it again.

Besides writing letters to family, friends, and fans, I read books like *The Art of War*, an ancient Chinese work considered a classic piece of military literature; *The 48 Laws of Power*, a book written in 1998 that has been compared to *The Art of War*; *The Shack*, a Christian novel; as well as various urban books and lots of magazines and business books. I once read a book in two days that was 480 pages. I never would have done that on the outside.

During my incarceration, I read more books than I had ever read in my life. I did more writing than I had ever done in my life, and I did more thinking than I had ever done in my life. I tried to stay sharp while I was in prison. I had a lot of idle time, but I didn't want to have an idle mind. So I read, and I also learned how to play chess, some card games, and dominoes.

There's one letter I'll never forget. It was the first letter Kijafa ever wrote me. At the bottom, it said, "PS: Do your time. Don't let the time do you."

From the moment I first heard those prison doors slam behind me, I began to turn back to God—praying, reading the Bible, and recommitting my life to Him.

The only thing I could do was to have faith and stay strong, and to trust and believe that God would give me another chance. It was all I had. There were so many times that He was the only person I could call on. I could talk to my mom, I could talk to Kijafa, I could talk to my kids; but I couldn't talk to them all night. You only get 300 minutes a month on the prison phones—an average of ten minutes a day—so you have to ration them out.

When I called Kijafa, I had so much on my mind that I wanted to tell her, and I'd have to cram it into five minutes.

I had to lie in that bunk in a cell by myself when the lights went out at 11:00—and I'm a night owl, so from 11:00 until 1:30 or until I fell asleep, I was thinking about how I could make this right. Those were lonely hours.

Just like high school, I read the Bible every night. My Bible, once again, found its place under my pillow. Scriptures from my childhood, like Psalm 23 and Jeremiah 29:11, began to bring me comfort again. It felt like I was starting my life all over again, only in a different place.

Some may question my sincerity or say, "Of course he found God in prison," as if it is a crutch or an excuse or an easy way to show remorse or reform. But in reality, I didn't find God; He found me. He put me in a place to be alone and to have conversation with Him. And I needed to listen.

As I look back on it, I had to come out of jail and take baby steps to get back to where I wanted to be. There was so much that needed to change, including breaking ties with longtime friends and associates who weren't the best influences on me in my pre-prison days.

God knew that I couldn't walk away from the dogfighting situation without my friends saying, "How are you just going to walk away from it? How are you not going to do this anymore?" God knew that in some ways I was arrogant, and He also knew that when I was younger, I used to pray. God gave me the strength to get through the prison sentence. He knew that I didn't have the strength to say no—that I didn't have the heart to tell people that they had to go their own separate way, that they couldn't be a part of my life anymore, that I needed to start a new life and it would be family-oriented—family first.

As I thought about it, I was reminded how I had lost sight of everything, of all the good people who helped me reach the pinnacle of my career. I just had no strength—no strength—to say no to those who were negatively influencing me. Being in that moment—being in that situation—was so surreal because I knew that what I had done and what I had worked for really didn't matter anymore.

As a part of the prison system, you almost feel like you're a nobody. You don't exist to the world at all. You're just a guy with a name and a number.

I had so much downtime when I was in prison, I had to think

about how I arrived at the point where I was. How did I reach a level of success that I had wanted and had always dreamed of? How could I resurrect all of that?

I thought about my walk with God and how I used to read the Bible when I was in high school. I thought about the steps I took to get to the NFL. And I thought about who was in my life that was most important. I realized that without God, I couldn't do it; and that without God, I couldn't get out of prison. He's not a crutch, a temporary fix; He is the rock.

⌒

In January 2008, I was transferred to the famed US penitentiary at Leavenworth, Kansas. I no longer lived alone in a cell, but was in a large pod with about fifty other men.

My character was tested almost as soon as I arrived at Leavenworth, when it was made to look like I had some contraband. A guard walked up to me and threw a whole half-ounce of tobacco at my foot, trying to get me in trouble. I snapped and lost my cool with everyone. I'm not that type of guy, but at that point, I was ready to fight. I didn't care. I couldn't believe I was being set up.

All the inmates were pointing to the guard, saying the guard did it. The guard ended up coming and apologizing to me. So from that day forward, I knew they were out to get me.

Because I failed a drug test a few months earlier, I hoped to participate in the facility's drug treatment program. Being in the program would allow me to be released from prison up to a year ahead of schedule. I was led to believe that I qualified for the program, but I never was actually admitted. Thus, I had to serve my full sentence. It was one of the most frustrating aspects of my stay at Leavenworth.

I wasn't looking for shortcuts; I knew that what I had done was inhumane and wrong. But I was disappointed because my attorneys and I believed I was fully eligible for the drug program and the possibility of early release.

Repeatedly, I would have interviews to enter the program, only to be rejected. I won't say I was treated differently. The guards treated me fairly—well, some did, and some didn't. I just don't think the prison officials wanted to let me go early. I think they wanted me to max out my time and show me they weren't going to do me any favors—that there weren't going to be any shortcuts and that I was going to do every day until the last day.

I think it was to make a statement. I don't believe it had anything to do with me personally, because when I was in prison, I wasn't a hardhead; I didn't give anyone trouble. I did get mad at myself for allowing this to happen to me and my family, and mad at the prison authorities for not letting me enter the drug program. But I never let myself get to a point where I was feeling depressed. I knew that wasn't my life. I knew I wasn't going to spend my whole life in prison. I couldn't fault the prison system—I shouldn't have put myself in prison in the first place. And if you're there, you have to abide by their rules.

I had a motto: "Tough times won't last, but tough people do."

No matter who was there or how much money they had on the outside, an inmate was only allowed $70 a week ($300 a month). We couldn't spend any more than that on things like phone calls and commissary purchases. Those are the parameters that you have to stay within. It was very humbling.

I had a job in the prison earning twelve cents an hour working as a late-night janitor, which fit well with my "night owl" ways. The entire compound was locked down, and everyone was asleep when I'd be up mopping the floor. I slept during the day. By the time I woke up, which was two or three o'clock in the afternoon, it was like the day had already passed. It helped the time go by and helped me through the tough times. It helped to keep me isolated.

At the end of the month, my check was $11. I took pride in it. I was happy because I earned it. Having a true blue-collar job was something I'd never experienced before. It was hard work. Every three months, we had to buff the floors and strip them—me and two other inmates I worked with. We took pride in doing it because we wanted to make sure it was done right. I am actually glad I had that experience; I appreciate what I get to do for a living so much more now.

Kijafa hung in there with me. She was so supportive in my journey through prison, and she pulled me through that whole situation. She came out to visit me and wrote me letters. She let me know she was thinking about me—which meant a lot because I knew she had every reason to leave.

Without her, I don't know how I would have made it through. She was my confidant. There were days when I was sad and I was down. She gave me a sense of belief and stayed optimistic. She kept believing, and that helped keep my spirits up. I just couldn't ask for a better person in my life. That continues to this day.

One of my most difficult days at Leavenworth came when Kijafa brought our two daughters and my son, Mitez, to visit for two days. We weren't able to spend time together the second day, a Monday, because prison officials canceled visitation.

I visited with my family on Sunday and looked forward to seeing them the next day. On Monday, I sat in a waiting area and— through glass windows—watched Kijafa drive up in a truck and then saw Mitez run across the street toward the door. Everyone looked happy. But because someone else created trouble, the officials canceled visitation for the day. There was no more visitation that week until the weekend. When they canceled visitation, man, I cried so hard. I was so mad.

It was early in my sentence, which made it harder to deal with. There was nothing I could do. I'll never forget that a prisoner named Mr. Harlin came and found me. He was in his fifties. We called him "Old G." There was nothing he could do to make me feel better, but he made me look at it from a realistic perspective: "It's their prison, and they can do whatever they want to do. You're in here, but you can't be mad at them. What are you going to do?"

It was one of the longest days of my life.

Your family is all you have when you're in prison. Other than that, it's like being dead.

The most difficult thing to deal with in prison was the death of my grandmother.

I remember calling my mother for her birthday. When she answered, I could hear a different tone in her voice.

"I wish I wouldn't have to tell you something like this in prison," she said, growing quiet, "but your grandmother is in the hospital. And it doesn't look good."

I dropped the phone.

Soon after, my grandmother died—the lowest moment of my time in prison. I'm still convinced that my grandmother's early departure from this earth is because of me—because of how heartbroken she was over my situation. The day I told her I was going to training camp—that was the last time I saw her.

What made it hurt even more was that I was not allowed to leave prison to attend her funeral.

It was devastating. I wanted to be there to support my family, but I couldn't. I was sitting in a jail cell.

Before I went to prison, I told my grandmother I was going to training camp. After the faith and the foundation she instilled in me, I couldn't bear to tell her the truth—that I was going to prison. And walking away from her house, I remember praying, "Please let me see my grandmother again."

But it'd be the last time I saw her.

In a way, however, God *did* answer that prayer. When I look at my youngest daughter, London, I see my grandmother. Now, I see my grandmother every day. I still can't believe London looks exactly like her. It's amazing. And it's a blessing that comes straight from God.

⌒

Twice, I was transported from Leavenworth back to Virginia for court hearings—first, for a state dogfighting case in November 2008, and later to appear in bankruptcy court in March 2009, less than two months before my release. (I'll describe how I got into money troubles in the next chapter.) Because of those times of transit, I spent time in eight different prisons, counting Northern Neck and Leavenworth. I spent short stints in two Petersburg, Virginia, facilities—one state and one federal; in Oklahoma City; in Suffolk (Virginia) Regional; in a small penitentiary in Leavenworth; and in the Atlanta Penitentiary. The various stops gave me a unique perspective on the diversity of prisons in America.

They all look different. They all have their own sort of serious mystique about them—their own personal feel—as you walk in. Yet all of them were just big and dirty. It was weird.

Some prisons, the inside may be green. In other ones, the inside may be orange. But they all had the same setup as far as the pods and the tiers. It was just scary, really scary. Those prisons were the worst.

It was kept private that I spent five days in the Atlanta Penitentiary—in my former NFL city—while in transit back to Leavenworth after my bankruptcy court hearing. My hands and feet were shackled for the bus ride from Petersburg to Atlanta, which lasted about eight hours. I'll never forget the Atlanta Penitentiary, seeing big rats running through it during the night. It was just nasty.

No matter the prison, they were all such unsanitary environments. There might be eighty guys sharing three bathroom stalls. It's uncomfortable, very uncomfortable. Roaches crawled on my bed and on me at night, and I had to sleep with earplugs and with a skull cap. There were mice under my bed. I had M&M's under my bed, and I had little mice eating my M&M's. I couldn't sleep for anything; it was impossible.

You heard those doors slamming all the time. But as loud as the doors were, and as unsanitary as the prisons were, I remember specific smells the most. If I smell a certain shampoo now, it brings back the memories.

It was only by the grace of God that I made it through all that and didn't break down. I knew I had to stay strong and stand tall for my family.

⌣

While at Leavenworth, I'd gather with other inmates in TV rooms and watch NFL games. Beforehand, we went to the commissary for pizza, chips, popcorn, and other game-day snacks, just like fans all over America. And that's what I was in those days—a huge fan.

What better way to spend time than watching the game you love? I'm a big fan of football, even when I'm not playing. I make my own evaluations of guys. It was sort of like being a coach.

Despite being in prison and unable to play in the NFL, it wasn't overly hard to watch the games—except for the fact that I was sur-rounded by a room full of self-proclaimed experts.

I laugh about that now, but those guys thought they knew what they were talking about—thought they knew more than me. Seri-ously, they were just an unbelievable group. Some of them had played some level of football before, and there were guys you never expected who knew a lot about football. Sometimes, I think they knew too much.

I would get hounded with questions. I found myself having to explain certain plays. Again, it was like being a coach, and it helped somewhat to keep my football mind sharp.

My friends and I also watched *106 & Park* every day, college football, *Dancing with the Stars*, *Entourage*, various documenta-ries, and *SportsCenter*. It's what guys do every day in prison. But that's a small glimpse of the good.

In the meantime, there's the bad. The crime. The danger. The rats. The roaches.

At least I had God and football.

~~

Despite the difficult environment, the people who befriended me, and those who I befriended, made it bearable. I hung out with Antoine from St. Louis, Cornell from Chicago, and Huey from New Orleans every day, and all three made me laugh, letting my mind escape for a while.

They were all guys who helped me get through. They helped me because each day is a struggle and is stressful. You just want to go home. You need people to pass the time with. You need people to walk on the track with. You have to be able to find ways to get through the tough times.

We found a way to make a positive out of a negative. We all kind of stuck together. We all ate together and lived the prison life together. Antoine and I would stay up for hours some nights, talking. We talked about what we were going to do, how we were going to live when we got out, and really just anticipated getting out.

I also did plenty of autograph signing for the other inmates and even for some of the guards—even though that wasn't supposed to happen. When I first came in, it was like, "No autographs!" If they caught anyone with my signature, they were going to consider it contraband. But when I left, I had eight or nine pieces of paper or memorabilia in my face, with guards asking me for my autograph.

ᴄᴄ

Despite playing in a prison basketball league and being in good enough shape to help my team to a championship, there was no way I could stay in NFL playing shape. But I tried to stay as fit as possible.

There were times at Leavenworth when I had access to weights and exercise equipment, but other times they weren't available—depending upon whether inmates were following the rules. Whenever someone got in trouble, those privileges would be taken away. It could be because of any incident. If someone got caught with alcohol or cigarettes, or if someone got caught with a cell phone, the item would be taken away—and everyone else's privileges along with it.

When I did have weights, I tried to do upper-body exercises and also squats to keep my legs in shape. We had to make a squat bench. When we had weights, we squatted. When we didn't have the weights because they'd been taken away, we started squatting with sandbags. Then they took the sandbags. We had to be creative to work out.

We also sometimes had access to two treadmills, and I regularly ran on those pretty intensely. I had to work my lower body, but I couldn't keep it in shape. No matter the obstacle, I always thought, *I'm still going to be one of the fastest quarterbacks in the league. When I get out, I'll have some time to get in shape.*

Most of the time I worked out with a guy named Dino. He was from Chicago, and there was a smile on his face at all times. Dino would liven up your day. He was around fifty years old—just a great guy. He would do anything for you.

He would drink diet sodas every day, and I started drinking them when I worked out too. My favorite was Diet Coke, and my favorite snack was grapefruit—not the typical food of an elite athlete, I know, but you take what you can get.

Overall, the food was bad. When I first went to prison, I lost twelve pounds. So, they had to up my portions. Some of us went on a no-carb diet and did a lot of abdominal work and had pictures taken of our abs. The pictures were hung in the commissary for a competition we came up with. Inmates had to pay six dollars anytime they wanted a photograph taken, whether it was with a family member, a friend, or just of themselves. But we never got our ab photos back, apparently because the prison officials didn't want guys taking their pictures with me. They didn't know who was going to sell them or what was going to happen.

Even though we never got our pictures, guys were ripped up. And I still had twelve-pack abs!

As much as I worked out, and as much as I believed I wouldn't get so far out of shape that I wouldn't be able to play in the NFL again one day, there were times I wasn't so convinced. Honestly, there were days—a lot of days—that I wondered if I would play again. However, I thought the prospect was good because I'd been put in the NFL substance abuse program by the league. I think they did that mainly because they believed I had a future in the NFL. But I didn't know when that future would be. Would it be 2009? Would it be 2010? I kept thinking, *My skills may erode by then.* I just didn't know what my future held, which made it hard sometimes to stay positive.

When I was a teen, my faith and relationship with God kept me focused. While in prison, I was blessed and fortunate to gain very strong support from a somewhat unexpected person: Tony Dungy.

I'm thrilled and honored that it didn't take Coach Dungy long to say yes when my attorney, Billy Martin, called to ask if he would visit me in Leavenworth. Coach Dungy and I had met in Japan nearly four years earlier in August 2005, when I was with the Falcons for a preseason exhibition against his Indianapolis Colts. We didn't get to spend a lot of time together in Japan, but we learned that we shared an interest in fishing and agreed to try to plan a get-together in the future.

The fishing expedition never happened, which Coach Dungy says he regretted, especially after my legal troubles began surfacing. Coach Dungy says it hurt him that we never got together to fish, because perhaps our conversation would have led to me sharing some of my problems with him. "That's what runs through your mind," he told me. "But it didn't happen. We missed our time."

As far as I was concerned, Coach Dungy's arrival at Leavenworth on May 5, 2009, was right on time. It came fifteen days before my scheduled release to home confinement and filled me with encouragement for my future, both in life and in football.

I was very excited and, at the same time, very nervous about him coming. I mean, this was Coach Dungy—a powerful man, very smart and humble—and I knew what his life was all about. I knew the principles he was dedicated to: he was a family man and a man of God.

When I went to the visitation area, I was dressed not as an NFL player but as an inmate wearing an orange jumpsuit. Coach Dungy says, however, that he was pleased with how he found me. This is what he told others about our experience together:

> I wanted to see if Michael looked like what I remembered, and he really did. He still looked like a young guy. He had bright eyes. He was excited, and he was looking

forward to getting out and bouncing back as a person and as a dad. Appearance-wise, he didn't look a lot different to me. That was refreshing to see.

I have been in a lot of prisons, so I wasn't shocked about the environment. Even for me, Leavenworth is a place you've heard about. It was kind of an awe-inspiring feeling to be there. He and I talked a lot about what it meant to be in prison. He came to the conclusion a lot of people come to—that when suddenly you don't have your freedom, you're not able to make decisions or communicate with people, and the things you took for granted, you don't take for granted anymore.

I think it was encouraging for Michael to see a football coach and be able to talk about football. It wasn't something he was able to do much during his time in prison.

Coach Dungy was right. I loved the visit so much that I didn't want him to leave.

I remember him looking into my eyes and wanting to know the truth about everything and how I felt. It was a special moment for me. *Why would Coach Dungy come all the way from his home in Tampa to visit me in Kansas?* I wondered. I knew there was a reason behind all of it, and I was just so thankful and delighted to be in his presence.

Coach Dungy says he remembers me being uncertain about whether NFL commissioner Roger Goodell would reinstate me and, if so, whether any teams would be interested. While Coach Dungy talked football with me, he tried to focus our conversation on a much broader scale, and we eventually came to the conclusion that the best thing for me was to continue turning my heart back to the Lord and make decisions that were best for my family. I needed to get my personal life, spiritual life, and family life back together—not worrying about the football side—because that would take care of itself if it was in God's plan.

In the months ahead, Coach Dungy became a close mentor to me. Because of what he heard and saw that day at Leavenworth, he says that he believed I was serious about changing my life. And I was. He felt like I was leaving prison as a different person.

Coach Dungy is one of the most widely respected sports figures in the nation, but his involvement with me drew criticism, including from some supporters of his Family First organization in Tampa. However, he says he was encouraged when he and his wife met an ex-convict working at a Tampa-area restaurant after word of his visit with me was publicized.

He and his wife were ordering take-out food, and the guy behind the counter told him, "I just have to tell you that I'm so happy with what you're doing with Michael, because I came out [of prison] four years ago and nobody would give me a chance. The only person who would was the owner of this restaurant, and I'm still here and still working hard for him. I just want to show him he did the right thing, and I'm not going to let him down. We need people to take a chance on us." This helped Coach Dungy know that he was doing the right thing. It didn't matter whether I would play in the NFL again. I was just a person who needed help launching a fresh start.

Let me tell you, Coach Dungy's visit and follow-up involvement with me were essential to my new beginning. Coach told me, "Walk out of here with your head up high. Walk out of here knowing that your future is bright and that you've got God on your side, and you'd better keep Him close."

When he said that, a totally different spirit overcame me.

⌒

Another special guest who visited me during the latter part of my stay at Leavenworth was Wayne Pacelle, the president and chief executive officer of the Humane Society of the United States.

I was surprised that he wanted to see me, considering the fact that two years earlier I had been viewed very negatively by his organization. I was nervous, but at the same time, excited to meet with him. I was also impressed with how sharp Wayne was and how he presented himself. I wasn't expecting to see the type of person I saw: he was clean-cut and came in with a suit on. Immediately, I thought he was a guy who was there to help.

His visit was a great opportunity for me to hear what the Humane Society was all about and to learn more about their mission and how I could potentially help. Right there in that prison visitation area, we forged a partnership. We agreed that once I was released, I'd begin to speak at Humane Society functions. Wayne told me he believed in me and that he was going to give me a chance to change a lot of lives of both people and dogs around the world—to change the perception of pit bulls and to help eradicate dogfighting. It was a great opportunity that I appreciated more than words can express.

⌁

The days seemed to get longer as the time drew near for my release to home confinement after eighteen months in prison. I could hardly wait for the day when I would be allowed to leave, and I frequently battled concerns that something would happen to prevent it.

I was so scared going down the stretch. Those were the slowest days ever. My friends inside prison helped me through those days and were sad to see me leave.

My fellow inmates and I had so much respect for each other. You get together every day. You develop bonds. You experience the same emotional roller coaster. One guy may be up one day and down the next, and you've got to keep his spirits up.

About two days before I expected to be released, I was startled when guards suddenly began a shakedown raid of the pod where I lived. They were looking for contraband or any sign of trouble. I had worked late and had just gone to bed.

I hurried to put clothes on so I could leave with the rest of the men, but was ordered by a guard: "You! Stay over there in the corner."

I was like, *Aw, what did I do?!* I was two days from going home, and I was afraid I had done something wrong. But it turned out to be a false alarm. They just held me back to tell me they were going to let me go a day earlier, to avoid the media and all that. I was allowed to call Kijafa, and she arrived the next day in time for me to make a 4:00 a.m. departure.

I used my last evening there to say good-bye to the friends I'd made and to exchange contact information with them for future reference—once we were all released and off probation.

The other prisoners were happy for me—happy that I was getting out, and happy that I was going home. I just wanted to make the most of my life going forward.

Most of the men were sleeping when I turned in my prison jumpsuit and was given civilian clothes that next morning. Kijafa was led to a special entrance, where I met her.

Kijafa says it was like a movie. She ran to me and hugged me. Everything felt right. We were together again—finally free.

And we quickly headed out for what would be close to a twenty-four-hour drive home to Virginia.

Chapter Nine

Mad Money

"The bottom line is, I just wasn't ready for it."

This wasn't Monopoly money anymore.

It's worth pausing from the story of my homecoming to reflect on one of the most profound things that happened while I was in prison—a personal bankruptcy that turned my financial world upside down.

Things were much different when I was released from prison than when I first went in. Some of it was my fault. Some of it was because people I trusted let me down.

It was the culmination of a larger economic crash that resulted from mismanagement, but also from the costly effects of my legal troubles. In a span of four years, I went from being the NFL's highest-paid player to an imprisoned ex-player filing for bankruptcy and having to reach out to former teammates for loans.

As a result, I look back and see myself as a cautionary example for other athletes who suddenly go from poverty to riches. The transition can be such a fleeting experience if sound money management, good stewardship, and trustworthy people aren't in place.

Even before I faced dogfighting charges, I struggled with how to handle millions of dollars. Sometimes I may have tried to do too much for other people. I meant well, but I probably shouldn't have taken out loans to purchase luxurious cars, houses, boats, and jewelry for family, friends, and myself.

The bottom line is: I just wasn't ready for it. I had all the money and all the cars, but I was giving away too much money. I was getting $500,000 checks each quarter from my endorsement deal with Nike, but by the end of the quarter, I was dipping into my bank account to pay bills because I had so many expenses.

I was at a point where I was starting to get worried: *Man, I can't have all these bills. I'm taking care of all these people. I have a house in Virginia, I have a house in Miami, I have my mom's house, I have my son's mom's house. I have, like, fourteen cars, paying car notes on all of them. That's $30,000 here, $40,000 there. I have a whole lot of other stuff I've been doing, and all types of bills coming in.* Every time I looked up, I was paying some sort of property tax.

Once I landed in prison, everything spiraled completely out of control, and I ended up filing for Chapter 11 bankruptcy protection. Eventually, I'll have to repay creditors around $20 million. But I felt that was better than filing for Chapter 7, because it shows accountability for my debts.

I just took my lawyers' advice in the situation and tried to do what was right. I didn't want it to seem like I was trying to stiff my creditors or anything like that, because I knew I owed them. I also knew I had a lot of assets I could liquidate as well.

～～

I don't want it to seem in any way that I'm bragging about money, but I think it's important to look back at the money I made in the NFL and what eventually happened to it.

I received an initial $3 million bonus upon signing my rookie contract with the Falcons. Four years later, I signed an eight-year extension on Christmas Eve that turned the revised contract into a ten-year, $130 million deal, making me the NFL's highest-paid player.

It was a huge contract. I had earned more than $7 million before I got that deal. It was what I made off my first rookie contract.

This was extra money for me. It was money I wanted to put away to be safe. I wound up investing it, but if I could do it all over again, I would have taken that money and just put it in a bank.

Things happen for a reason, though. While my legal troubles took a toll, I still had a lot of money to pay off creditors and money that I had borrowed from banks. It would've been more than enough. I could've served my prison sentence and never filed bankruptcy—if I had just put the money in the bank like I had planned and not invested it.

I was only twenty-four at the time of the big contract, just six years out of high school. The money made me an easy target for family and friends looking for helpful handouts, and there was plenty to go around. In my heart, I wanted to help them, but I realize it became excessive.

You have to remember that we grew up with next to nothing. When I think about my past, my upbringing, living in public housing, and how hard my mom and dad worked to make ends meet, my main objective was to bless them as much as I could. I wanted to let them enjoy life. I wanted to let them have a chance to catch their breath.

Yes, I would say I did too much for too many people. I spoiled them. However, a lot of my friends did come to me with business ideas. They had a lot of bright ideas, but I just wasn't mature and ready for them.

It was partly my fault, because I would much rather just give them money than let them go out and take the necessary steps to start a promising business venture on their own—mainly because it was going to cost more money to invest in the types of projects they wanted to do, including paying salaries. Plus, I was scared of them not succeeding.

Sometimes I look at my imprisonment and bankruptcy from a spiritual perspective. As I've said previously, I believe God wanted to lovingly but firmly get me on course for a more successful life. I think it was just God's way of saying, "You're doing it all wrong, son."

It was like He was saying, "I love you too much to see you end your career and end up broke. I love you too much to have you go out in the wee hours of the night in one of these dogfights and get shot. I love you too much for you not to carry out My plan. There's so much more for you down the road that you can't see. You don't know, but I know."

My finances became so tight when I was in prison that I had to reach out to three former NFL teammates for loans. They knew the type of person I truly was, and they knew I was in a situation I had to bounce back from. It wasn't like I was asking for $100,000 or anything like that. It was just enough to get by—enough to get me home and get me through the bankruptcy.

Not only did teammates help me financially, but they helped me emotionally as well.

Joe Horn, who previously played for Falcons' rival New Orleans before joining Atlanta in 2007, called me frequently to offer encouragement and support. He was calling me every day during my case, saying, "I'm here for you. I'll be here for you. I'll support you. You can get through it." And he helped me through.

⌒

My finances dwindled away in prison to the point that my debts were bigger than my assets. One major reason for this was the access I gave others to my investments and money while incarcerated.

I never spent all the money I had earned in my career. I admit that I spent a lot, but I had a lot. The amount that went out was nowhere near the amount that came in.

Much of my money was tied up in real estate, and I had asked my financial advisor at the time to sell it, but he would not liquidate the property because of the recessed market and because he had his own money tied up in it. I had more than $6.5 million invested in real estate. But he wouldn't sell. It's as though he never even cared about the fact I needed that money to help settle some financial issues.

When you're in a situation where you need a helping hand and you need people to be there for you—people you can rely on and trust—the true person comes out. Those types of situations show you a different side of those around you, because you're down and your back is against the wall, and you need them the most. You learn that sometimes people don't care about you as much when you don't have anything to offer. It wasn't just my financial advisors. I also allowed family and friends access to my money, and their spending contributed to my demise too.

If you go out and mismanage your money and you place it in bad investments, but you do it yourself, then you only have yourself to blame when you take a loss. I'd rather not blame someone else for how they managed my money, because in reality, it was ultimately my responsibility.

Not everything was as bad as it looked, though.

There were some things that emerged in bankruptcy court filings that were very misleading, including a $1,000 check from me to my mother that had "chump change" written on the memo line. It's not like it sounds. Our family did not take money for granted. My mom wrote that on the check, not me. (She would write checks, and I'd approve them or sign them.) She wasn't trying to be arrogant or anything like that; it was just her way of being humorous. And she thought, *Who else is going to see it?* Nobody would have ever known if the documents had not been revealed in the bankruptcy case.

Based on the bankruptcy documents I had to file, there were also media reports saying I purchased a Mercedes Benz worth more than $90,000 on the day I turned myself in to prison. I did buy the car, but the timing of the purchase was reported incorrectly. It was totally false.

Why would I go buy a car the day I'm going to prison—one of the saddest days of my life? Material things don't bring you joy, and that certainly wasn't going to help my emotions at that time. I bought the Mercedes about three weeks earlier, downsizing from a 2007 Bentley Flying Spur that originally cost nearly twice as much ($160,000). I realize that may not seem like "downsizing," especially with the way things were with the economy, but given my income, it was downsizing for me.

Looking back, it's easy to see how someone could have inferred that my family and I were living and spending excessively. We didn't try to hide it. In the fall of 2006, I appeared on the cover of *Celebrity car* magazine's celebrity automobiles issue. In the article, I proudly proclaimed that I had the Flying Spur, a Bentley Coupe, a Benz, and a 2006 Navigator. I also pointed out that my mother had more cars than I did, including a Cadillac XLR convertible. Later on, after my legal troubles began, we needed to get rid of many of our assets. It was difficult, but I knew if I could play football again, I might be able to earn some of it back.

Having to get rid of assets was somewhat ironic because my mom was wanting to downsize her house anyway. These circumstances gave her the opportunity to do that and move into the house I was living in. Meanwhile, my son's mom moved out of the house she was living in because she wanted to live closer to Mitez's school. I also owned two boats—one in Miami and one in Virginia. I wasn't going back to Miami anytime soon because I had sold my condo down there. So I got rid of the boats because I wasn't going to use them. Those were my assets.

The whole process changed my ways and habits regarding cars especially. I used to drive them only a few months before trading them in, but then I gained some perspective on things, like the sales tax you have to pay on each car. Now, I am practicing greater moderation with cars and driving them much longer.

I guess when the story came out, everyone looked at it like my family and I really didn't care about money and didn't respect the situation we were in. It wasn't that way at all. We were grateful and thankful for everything we had. My mom always told me to be grateful each and every day. My grandmother told me that too. It was just a bad situation.

Despite all of my financial immaturity and mistakes, I believe bankruptcy could've been avoided if certain people overseeing my assets had done some of the things I asked, like liquidating some of my real estate investments in order to pay off debts. If I could start over, I would put all my money in the bank so I would know where it was. If I wanted to invest my money in something, I would have it in CDs, mutual funds, and maybe in real estate. This way, if I had to take a loss, I would take it based on *my* decisions and what *I* did—not because of someone else's decision.

Promising young athletes entering the NFL and other pro sports need to be mindful that there are "sharks" trying to take advantage of them and their money. The bottom line for me, given what I know now, is for the player to take a hands-on approach with his finances. Don't pay a financial advisor to hold your money. The bank will pay you to hold your money—it's called interest. So, your money is safe and making money, and it's not a high risk.

However, I've had some advisors that I still like and trust. One advisor really had my best interests at heart. He did a great job because all my money was accounted for. But you should never give anyone full access to your funds like I did. This advisor knew that other advisors and various people were talking to me, but he ended the relationship because he said that I refused to listen to his advice. I admit that I had a lot of people in my ear, and eventually I parted ways with the man.

I put a lot of trust in another financial advisor I had. I don't know enough to say for certain whether all of what he did was right or wrong. What I can say is this: I felt like he abandoned me when I needed his help the most. Things he did concerned me based on what I discovered through the bankruptcy process. He had my money invested in three different real estate projects—which included a lot of property, a lot of land, and two restaurants in Atlanta. There was money that never really was totally accounted for.

I wrote him several letters—stern letters—demanding that he turn over my money to a certain individual, that he liquidate all the assets and liquidate the investments. I knew I was going to take a loss, but having something was better than having nothing in terms of a judgment I needed to pay off. I just wanted to show people my honest desire to fulfill my obligation to pay back the money I borrowed from them.

Through it all, this financial advisor never came to see me in Leavenworth, never got on my visitors' list, never came out to ask what I needed or what he or his firm could do. He knew everything that was going on. But he never made the effort to come see me or contact me to talk about my financial situation. I should have been given all the information regarding what was going on. And I wasn't.

The fact that he never came to Kansas to see me hurt me more than anything else. I put an enormous amount of trust in him. He had received at least $7 million in cash from me, maybe even more than that. I never saw it again or even heard about what happened to that money until I went through bankruptcy.

I met this advisor back in January of 2005 through someone I feel very close to and still love—someone I had a lot of trust in and still have a lot of trust in to this day. I don't want to reveal that person's name, but because of that friend, I placed my trust in this financial advisor and believed he would have my best interests at heart. But in the end, that may or may not have been the case.

My relationship with him was great until I went to prison. That's when things changed. Leading up to prison, things kind of got out of whack when I started making certain demands for lump sums of my money, and the decisions I was making were being questioned. But I was doing it in my own best interest.

Before prison, this advisor and I met about once a month, and he would send me monthly financial reports. It's why I was so surprised that he acted the way he did and didn't communicate with me when I went to prison. To this day, I wonder what the reason was behind it. I haven't gotten an explanation for it. But I know now that he may have been leery of another person working with me—another financial advisor who was later sent to prison.

I guess he didn't trust this other person when they were making demands for large amounts of my money. But I gave this person orders to do so.

Maybe he saw potential problems and was trying to protect me. Maybe that was the reason, but no one told me. Still, there was no reason for him to seemingly disappear.

⌐⌐

Ultimately, in 2009, a bankruptcy judge ordered me to follow the advice of a court-appointed financial consultant and repay my creditors $20 million. That's also when I had to surrender my assets, like the boats and houses. I was put on a budget. For example, in 2010, I was given $300,000 to live on out of my $5.2 million salary with the Philadelphia Eagles. I don't mind living on a budget. It has helped me develop a better understanding about material things.

Money is still important. It's going to be important; you can't live without it. But I don't dwell on how much money I lost—particularly because I know I didn't spend it all, and I didn't put it all in jeopardy. I just look at it as making poor decisions in picking people to manage my money.

I don't live my life or play the game of football saying, "I need to make this much money." I think about enjoying what I do, achieving success personally and professionally, then maybe the money comes later. I think you need that type of attitude, and within those guidelines, things happen.

Most of all, more than ever, I've come to understand that money comes from God as a blessing, and I need to be a good steward of what He gives me.

Part III:

The Redemption

Chapter Ten

Coming Home

"I became focused on being a family man."

F ree from Leavenworth, I was thrilled by the simplest sights as Kijafa and I drove home to Hampton, Virginia. It was one of the best days of my life—May 20, 2009.

Being on the open road after eighteen months in prison—simply seeing McDonald's and hotels—was like living a brand-new life. It was awesome. For almost two years, I was a caged bird. Now, I was free.

My probation officer called and asked us to drive straight home, which would take almost a full day. Already, my house in Virginia was surrounded by media awaiting my return.

I decided against the option to fly home or ride a bus, so Kijafa and I took turns driving. It went faster than you'd think. I was just so excited to get behind the wheel of a car. I wanted to do something different. I wanted to get away—to see the world, the trees, the interstate, and stop signs. I had to free up my mind and just enjoy life again.

In prison, I was so limited in the time I could talk with Kijafa, whether it was on the phone or during her twice-a-month visits. But now we had what seemed like endless time to share our thoughts and hearts with each other. We talked about me coming home and seeing our daughters and my son—the chance to get to know London, our youngest daughter, and to see how she would respond. I wondered if she would be receptive to me.

We talked about the jobs that were part of my release program— about me doing construction for a few weeks and going to work at the Boys & Girls Club. I knew the construction job was going to be different. It was going to be a humbling experience.

While driving through Indiana, we got out of the car and gazed at a cornfield in the middle of nowhere—just to look at things. Freedom felt so good.

I was intrigued just to be in the car again. It was great to work a CD player and listen to music. It was nice to find out what was going on in the world, in Kijafa's family and in my family—just things that were important. At the same time, I was in disbelief that I was out. I said to myself, *I can't believe I'm free! I can't believe I'm free!*

Part of that freedom brought the opportunity to enjoy certain types of food—fun food—things I hadn't been able to eat in almost two years. Our first stop was a Pizza Hut in St. Louis. I ordered a pizza with cheese only. I like it plain. Later, we stopped at a Dairy Queen for a hot dog with chili, onions, ketchup, mustard, and relish—with French fries, of course. And the trip wouldn't have been complete without a visit to McDonald's, where I ordered a Big Mac.

⌒

Kijafa kept getting phone calls on our trip back.

"Do you know what your house looks like outside?" friends asked, referring to the television trucks, reporters, and cameras sitting in the cul-de-sac in front of the house.

"I can only imagine," she said. "I can only imagine."

When we arrived, we had to pull right into the garage to dodge the media circus. I walked into the house and saw my daughters. I hadn't seen them in six months. It was an extraordinary moment.

Jada ran into my arms. "My baby!" I said, picking her up. "I missed my baby." To be reunited with her seemed like I never left. She was three when I left and five when I came home.

London—who was two at the time—was only a month old when I went to prison, so she had no experience of me living at home as her father. It took her a few days to warm up to the idea. I had seen her only about five times during prison visits.

She was scared of me at first. She had only seen me behind the glass, and she would kiss the glass. Now, she didn't even recognize me. For the first two days, she didn't want to come to me. Kijafa was sad about it and cried. I remember picking London up when I first saw her, pointing at myself, and saying, "My daddy. My daddy," trying to tell her who I was.

I figured it would just take time. It's like taking a child who's used to being in one house, and you put her in another house around a totally different group of people. She's going to be shy unless she's extremely outgoing. It's just the way it is. Still, we wondered if I could ever make up for the two years of absence in her life.

I had to talk to her, kiss her, and let her know that Daddy was home. After about two days, I was chasing the kids around the house—not pushing London too much, just giving her space, but at the same time letting her know that I'm her daddy and that I love her. I'll never forget it; out of the blue, out of nowhere, she said, "I missed you, Daddy. Daddy, I missed you."

She basically told me everything she had been feeling. She knew who I was. She didn't hear anyone else say that; it came from her. Right then and there, I resolved, *I can never leave my family again.* When London realized I was her father, it was one of the greatest moments of my life. This was where I was supposed to be.

It was great being around close friends again, like my pastor, Domeka Kelley. He visited me when I was at the Warsaw Regional Jail, and we wrote one another while I was in Kansas.

He has always looked out for what God wanted in my life. He was thrilled I was home, but he also knew it would be tough.

Pastor Kelley said in an interview: "I wanted [Michael] home, but I knew it was going to be a difficult road ahead of him. We live in a cruel world. I can't expect everyone to be forgiving. I knew society wasn't going to welcome him back or embrace him because of the mistakes he made. By the grace of God, he made it. One thing about Michael, he is tough."

Being with Pastor Kelley in those early days after my release was key for me in my faith journey as I transitioned from being in prison to being back home. He gave me a Bible, one called a parallel Bible because it has two versions—in this case, the King James Version and the Amplified Bible—presented side-by-side so you can compare how the verses were translated. It meant a lot that he gave it to me and wanted me to believe it and understand it. He just wanted me to get closer to God. I try my best to read it regularly, and I can call him if I need help understanding something. Pastor Kelley likes to say we "dive" into the Scripture in order to gain a deep and lasting understanding.

He says he looks back on my life and thinks about the verse that says, "It is easier for a camel to go through the eye of a needle, than for a rich man to enter into the kingdom of God" (Matthew 19:24 KJV). He understood the temptations I faced on a daily basis and the challenges that came with living a life in the spotlight.

I love Pastor Kelley. He has invested so much in me, my family, and my relationship with God. Like Coach Dungy, he has believed in me. I can tell you without a doubt that my faith in God is what's gotten me through everything I've endured.

Two months of home confinement was much better than prison. I liked being in the house. I could stay in the house all day and find a ton of things to do with my kids. My friends and brother would come over, and we would have a good time. But, make no mistake about it, it was confining.

I was only able to leave the house for work. I worked the construction job for about three weeks and later worked about three weeks more at a local Boys & Girls Club. I was getting paid and then donating the money right back to the Boys & Girls Club. It's something I enjoyed and still enjoy doing. And it was only fitting to be starting all over at the place that changed my life to begin with. Because of Mr. James "Poo" Johnson, my life stayed on the right track when I was younger, while so many of my peers strayed. And here we were again. Mr. Johnson and I were together.

Hoping I could soon return to the NFL, I exercised during my confinement in an upstairs workout room. But it was far from what pro football players are used to using. I weighed about 225 pounds when I got out of prison—about fifteen to seventeen pounds more than my normal playing weight. I really couldn't do much at the house. The room was so small, and I didn't have free weights like I prefer to use. I had an elliptical machine, a treadmill, and an ab lounger. I'd run on the treadmill and break a sweat, but I couldn't open up a sprint, couldn't run outside, and couldn't get my body in tip-top shape.

During those two months, I was required to wear an ankle bracelet that allowed probation officers to monitor my location at all times. Other than when specifically permitted, such as going to work, I wasn't allowed to venture beyond about a fifty-yard radius around the house.

The monitor on my ankle bracelet was extremely accurate. On the last night before my home confinement ended, I was on the sidewalk talking to friends, and I apparently drifted just past the boundary. My probation officer called and asked, "Why did Mike just leave the house? Why is he out of range right now?" But I was standing right there! It got real sensitive toward the end of my confinement. I couldn't wait to be done with that little machine.

I enjoyed being home, but home confinement is truly home confinement. You can't leave to go anywhere except for work—not even to the store to get a gallon of milk.

⌐⌐

Perhaps the greatest blessing for me after my release from prison was getting reacquainted with my family.

It felt like I never left. All we did was bond. I was determined never to return to the wild, partying ways that eventually landed me in trouble in Atlanta.

Just the memory of having to leave my family in the first place was so sobering. It was very hard when I left for prison because London had just been born. She was only one month old, and I can't get those two beautiful years back. I was leaving Kijafa, who'd had a C-section, and it was hard for her to get around. I was leaving Jada, my oldest daughter, who I helped Kijafa care for as a newborn. And I was leaving Mitez—whose heart was broken when he saw his father's potential prison sentence come on the television. I knew what I was leaving behind. Being reunited was extra-special.

Like Coach Dungy advised, I became focused on being a family man.

The children caused me to slow my life down. They mean more to me than anything else in this world. If I have something to get done, or if I have an obligation, I primarily want to make sure I spend quality time with them first. It's important to me because my schedule is often overbooked and busy. I want them to know I can't be there all the time, but I'm doing the best I can. I put them first.

My life now is focused around family, and I love my family members. Each one of them is unique. Each relationship is very important to me and has been crucial to my development as a man.

Now I strive to be the man God called me to be; not for myself, but for them. It is more important to be a husband and father than it is for me to be a football player. For them, I will be the strong leader of my house that I needed to be before my troubles began.

Coming home wasn't just about getting out of prison and back to Virginia; it was more than that. It was about returning to the foundations of my life—faith and family.

Chapter Eleven

Starting Over

"I had no margin for error."

Once my home confinement ended, I nervously awaited meeting with NFL commissioner Roger Goodell concerning my possible reinstatement to the league. I deeply regretted lying to him about my involvement in dogfighting, and I looked forward to having an opportunity to make amends and regain his confidence.

The opportunity came one week after my federal sentence was completed.

I was so excited to see him and talk to him again, to apologize face-to-face, and to try and reconcile our relationship and the credibility I'd had with him at one time. I had spent so many countless hours thinking about what I would say and how I would approach the entire conversation.

I went into the meeting with this whole dissertation of what I wanted to say—things like, "I'm sorry, and I should've told the truth" or "I was involved, and I feel so bad because I let a lot of people down, including you."

But the first thing Commissioner Goodell said was, "We're not here to talk about the past. We're here to talk about how you're going to change your life moving forward—how you're going to better yourself and correct all the mistakes you made and how we can prevent you from going down that path again."

When I saw the look in his eyes—the intensity in his face—and heard what he was saying, I knew he was in my corner. I didn't know exactly how I would be reinstated, but I realized I had the chance to rebuild myself, my image, and my self-confidence.

Initially, I was reinstated only for the preseason, with the possibility of missing the first few weeks of the regular season. (That would later change.) Nevertheless, I was thrilled to have a chance to sign with an NFL team again.

⌒

The chance that a team might want me and take the risk on me was greatly enhanced by Coach Dungy's unwavering support. He encouraged teams to sign me, and he served as an advocate for me.

Coach put his name and reputation on a kid—a man—who was coming out of prison and didn't know what direction his professional career would take him. Coach Dungy basically reached out to Commissioner Goodell and to a couple of teams, and said, "Believe in this guy. I'm sending him to you with my blessings. Trust him."

Without Coach Dungy, it probably wouldn't have worked; I probably wouldn't have been reinstated. I needed a prominent figure who had integrity, respect, and the spiritual blessings to help me get a job in the NFL.

Coach promoted me despite receiving criticism for doing so.

When Coach Dungy spoke out for me, this is what he told people:

> I think Mike understands about having Christ in his life, and that God has given him this second chance. As much as he doesn't want to let me or other people down, he doesn't want to let the Lord down again. I really believe that.
>
> That was one of the reasons I didn't feel I was taking a gamble or going out on a limb. I felt like he was going to come out and do the right things. I had no idea if he would get his athleticism back and be able to play quarterback, but I didn't worry about him going down the wrong path once he got out.

My agent, Joel Segal, told me Buffalo and Cincinnati were interested in signing me. But it came as a big surprise when I was informed that Philadelphia was strongly in the mix too. The Eagles already had my friend Donovan McNabb as their starter, plus a talented young backup, Kevin Kolb, a second-round draft pick in 2007.

Even though Philadelphia was already loaded at quarterback, it actually was a better situation for me than Buffalo. The Bills would have been screaming for me to play immediately, and I knew I wasn't ready or in shape to do that yet. Because I was fresh out of prison and no one knew what the public's reaction would be, it probably would have been a bad deal to put me in a situation where I was going to have to play immediately. We were all conscious of that.

More important to my comeback than public opinion was my need to get in football shape: it was huge. Remember, I weighed 225 pounds instead of my usual 208 to 210.

The Eagles kept their interest in me top secret. My close friend CJ Reamon and I drove to Philadelphia from Virginia and stayed overnight at the home of Eagles owner Jeffrey Lurie after first meeting with team president Joe Banner. I played a game of chess with Mr. Lurie's son and also talked with Mr. Lurie's wife, Christina.

My interview with Mr. Lurie was very intense. He has a way of asking you questions and trying to get a read on you and what you're thinking. He really grilled me—wanting to know if I was sincere, if I wanted to take advantage of my second chance, and if I was serious about football this time around.

I could tell the Eagles put a lot of thought into it. I didn't expect it to be easy, and it wasn't.

They were sticking their necks out for me and didn't want me doing anything to smack them in their faces. They told me, "Don't embarrass the organization." I made them a promise that I wouldn't.

The next morning, I signed a one-year contract with an option for a second year.

Once again, I was part of an NFL team.

It was great because I had no pressure on me. The Eagles were just going to mix me in with a couple of packages and give me time to get myself in shape. What more could you ask for?

This time around, I knew I would give anything for the organization that I belonged to.

After a press conference, I reported to practice, taking the field for the first time in more than two years. It was so gratifying to have a new opportunity to play in the NFL. Eagles coach Andy Reid took particular interest in my recovery because his own sons, Garrett and Britt, were imprisoned on drug-related charges in 2007. I think Coach Reid totally understands the meaning of a second chance. Most people don't have to experience walking into a prison and seeing their son or daughter incarcerated.

You just see so many guys locked up, enduring wasted lives and idle time. If you know that individual and you know their heart and what type of effect they can have out in society, then you have a little sympathy for them. I think that was the situation with Coach Reid. He understood I was a good person, a good kid, and all I wanted to do was play football. I just got caught up doing the wrong things. Not just dogfighting, but everything else that came along too.

My signing was met with mixed reactions from Philadelphia fans. Some supported me, while others blasted the move, including the owner of a sandwich shop who vowed never to serve me food. But you know what? People have said so many things about me that it doesn't even bother me when they say negative stuff—unless it's something I know is absolutely not true.

But not everyone had negative feelings toward me. I found two great places to have a cheesesteak: Pat's King of Steaks and Jim's Steaks. The first time I visited Jim's, they recognized me and gave me a cheesesteak on the house.

⌒

Shortly after signing with the Eagles, I was photographed having a drink in the bar of a Philadelphia hotel. It stirred media speculation about whether I had violated my probation.

I was meeting with James DuBose, who was producing *The Michael Vick Project* documentary for BET. We were just sitting there, having a nice conversation, talking about how we were going to present the documentary to the world. I had a Grey Goose and pineapple. At the time, as a twenty-nine-year-old man, I felt like if I wanted to mellow out and just relax, I could have a drink.

When I left the bar, I got on the elevator, not knowing a beat writer or a sportswriter had gotten on with me. He had seen me down in the restaurant, so he went there to find out what I ordered and what I was drinking. He wrote in the paper that I was having a conversation with another guy and also having dinner with a mixed drink. He tried to find out if that was a violation of my probation. That's how far he took it.

I didn't know whether it was personal or whether people just didn't want to see me succeed. But why would someone take it so far to see if it was a violation of my probation?

Even though I felt I had done nothing wrong, Coach Dungy let me know I needed to be more careful and use better judgment. Coach said I had to be conscious of what I was doing. I had to be conscious of where I was and realize that I couldn't do certain things I had done before, like having a casual drink at a bar. Now, I was under the microscope.

I had no margin for error.

Two weeks after signing with the Eagles, I played in my first NFL exhibition game in three years.

The day of my Philadelphia debut, August 27, 2009, was exhaustingly full for me. I traveled to Newport News, Virginia, during the day to participate in my bankruptcy settlement hearing and then arrived back in Philadelphia for the game. The judge approved a $20 million settlement for me to repay my creditors over a six-year period.

On the field that night, I appeared in six plays, including one as a slot receiver and another when I completed a pass right-handed. I was 4-of-4 passing for 19 yards.

"It's been a long journey for me," I told the media afterward. "I just want to do it right this time around."

Philadelphia fans are stereotypically brutal and unforgiving, but that night, I received a standing ovation when I entered the game and even heard "We want Vick!" chants as I walked off the field. I listened for the reaction when I ran on the field at the start of the game and was very humbled and thankful to receive a warm welcome. I didn't expect it.

Once the regular season arrived, I played sparingly, mostly as a Wildcat quarterback to either run the ball or serve as a running decoy. For the season, I completed 6-of-13 passes for 86 yards and one touchdown, and rushed 23 times for 95 yards and two touchdowns. Two of the touchdowns—one rushing and one passing—came in a reunion game in Atlanta against the Falcons.

Playing against Atlanta was bittersweet. It was weird taking the same road I had always taken to the stadium. And I shed a tear because that was once my home. That was my city. That was my team. And here I was—once a starter, playing my old team as a third-string quarterback.

It was humbling for me and taught me that you can't take life for granted. If there's an opportunity and you can put yourself in the driver's seat, it's happening for a reason, and it's a gift from God. I had an opportunity in Atlanta, and I threw it down the drain.

I felt like I had a lot to clear up in Atlanta. I love that city, and it felt like I left so suddenly. I dropped by an Atlanta radio station a day before the big game. I wanted to apologize for what happened and speak to the city.

Radio host Ryan Cameron's son asked me a question during the interview. "Did you think about your fans when you were dogfighting?" the little boy asked.

"To answer your question," I said, "I really wasn't thinking about anybody but myself, which is selfish. I didn't care about anybody else's feelings; I only cared about mine. I made a bad decision and [used] bad judgment at the most important time in my life."

"You never said a proper good-bye," Ryan commented toward the end of the interview.

"I wish I could turn back the hands of time," I told him. "Wish I could do it all over again and do it the right way. I just want people to know—all the people that will be in that dome tomorrow—that I appreciated every moment, every cheer, every outcry. I just hope everybody can forgive me, and if not, I understand."

I signed off, saying, "ATL, I love you, baby."

It was true. I will forever love that city.

Really, the only other notable thing I did that season on the field was complete a 76-yard pass to wide receiver Jeremy Maclin in a playoff loss against the Dallas Cowboys. At the time, it was the longest scoring pass of my career.

At the conclusion of the season, I was extremely honored that my Philadelphia teammates voted to give me the team's Ed Block Courage Award. And during Super Bowl week in Miami, I was invited to speak with Coach Dungy at an Athletes in Action ministry event. It gave me an opportunity to share my testimony about how God had given me a second chance in life and how I was trying hard to make the most of it.

Overall, my first year back in the NFL was like my redshirt year at Virginia Tech all over again. I could have been a starter elsewhere, but it wouldn't have been what was best for me. I wasn't ready physically or mentally. I didn't know the Eagles' offense. And

I didn't have the confidence I needed to excel. But the Eagles gave me an opportunity to work hard and get my legs back in shape. Like Virginia Tech, that year helped prepare me.

It helped prepare me for another takeoff.

Chapter Twelve

A Crucial Offseason

"I just wanted Commissioner Goodell to know I'm a man of my word."

There were times in the months between the 2009 and 2010 seasons when I wondered if the Eagles would keep me—or if I'd be allowed to stay in the NFL.

It was an eventful and pivotal offseason—a time when I worked harder than ever to get into the best shape possible, but also when there was plenty of speculation that I could be traded away from Philadelphia. I also made a summer misjudgment that I feared had put my career in jeopardy again.

One of my codefendants in the dogfighting case, Quanis Phillips, was shot some time after a verbal altercation with me at my thirtieth birthday party in June.

I wasn't present at the time of the early-morning shooting, and I eventually was cleared of any wrongdoing, so I wasn't further disciplined by the NFL. However, I put myself in a very vulnerable situation, and the incident made me more committed than ever to avoid even a hint of trouble.

The original plan for the birthday party seemed harmless. My mother and Kijafa were going to host a private event for family members and close friends. However, I agreed to allow my brother, Marcus, to plan the event instead and make it open to the public for a cover charge.

I was trying to help Marcus make some money. We had hoped to profit somewhere between $10,000 and $12,000. I wasn't even going to make anything off it. Marcus was simply trying to get independent and make his own money.

We were actually planning to have three or four similar parties after that. But that never happened, of course, because the first one turned out to be a near-disaster.

For starters, Quanis and I were not supposed to be in one another's company since, as codefendants, we both had served time for felonies and were still on probation. Prior to that night, I hadn't even seen him for about seven or eight months. There really wasn't a friendship while we were on probation; we stayed away from each other and avoided any dealings with each other, understanding that it's better to keep it that way.

I arrived late for the party at Guadalajara Restaurant in Virginia Beach and only stayed for about an hour. I saw that Quanis was there, and we exchanged only a wave and a nod from a distance.

Later, after the singing of "Happy Birthday," Kijafa playfully put some birthday cake on my lips, much like what happens at wedding receptions. I was embarrassed and overreacted.

Okay, it was funny, but I was like, "Why would you do that in front of all these people?" For whatever reason, I was irritable that night, and it made me mad. Then she did it to one of my friends and I said, "All right, Kijafa, let's stop."

But that's when Quanis snuck up behind Kijafa, took some cake from her, and put it on my face. He had been drinking, and it was more cake than she had put on my face. It was a little too much. I was upset. I had some words with him and told him that I was basically ten seconds from jumping on him. But I calmed myself down and went away to sit in the car for a minute.

Kijafa got in the car and I told her to pull away. Then I told her to stop the car because my father was there, and I wanted to make sure he had a ride. I got out and, as I was walking toward the club, I saw a fistfight involving Quanis and one of Marcus's friends.

People thought I was coming back to fight, so everybody rushed me to try to calm me down. I told them, "Hold up; get your hands off me! I'm not coming to fight anybody. I know if I get in a fight out here, it's going to be on the five o'clock news tomorrow." I understood the consequences from a public standpoint, especially because it was at a nightclub, so I calmed everyone down, got in the car, and we pulled off.

Several minutes after that, Quanis was shot.

When I met with the police the next day, they saw everything on the footage from a video camera, including me leaving. Only about four minutes after I pulled off, another crew of guys came into view of the camera. They were fighting. You don't see anyone get shot. You just see two cars pull up next to each other, with one car pulling off, and another car pulling up, supposedly to shoot a guy.

I received a call on my cell phone about the shooting approximately fifteen minutes after it happened. I knew at that point it was going to be a long two or three weeks.

For days, I was in tears over the ordeal, including the next day at a youth football camp I was leading in Virginia Beach. I thought, *Man, I'm starting all over again. What a setback.* There were stories in the media about the Eagles letting me go. I felt like, *You're talking about cutting me? Who's going to pick me up knowing I'm going through this?*

So now I was thinking about my family and how I let them down. I was just so hurt, I can't even explain the feeling. I was older and more mature; I had come back and given everyone my word, looked them in the eyes, and said, "You can count on me." That's why it hurt.

I had a difficult conversation with Eagles coach Andy Reid about the incident. He told me he couldn't predict how the situation would go or what NFL commissioner Roger Goodell might do about it.

Commissioner Goodell had been complimentary about the changes I had been making. He would text me or call me randomly—just to see how I was doing. He even checked on me once when I was injured. I appreciated that. There's nothing like being able to pick up the phone and call the commissioner when you feel like things are in turmoil and not going your way, or when you see a potential problem.

Commissioner Goodell is a great friend who cares about you and your family. He only wants to see you excel. I made a promise to him, and I'll never forget what was said at the conclusion of our roundtable meeting back when I was reinstated. It was Commissioner Goodell, a couple of his representatives from the NFL, Senior Vice President of Law and Labor Policy Adolpho Birch and the entire NFL group, along with me, my agent, and my lawyers. We all sat down at the table and had a four- or five-hour discussion.

At the conclusion of the meeting, Commissioner Goodell asked me out of the blue, "Without preparing a statement or having time to think about what you want to say, what are your expectations for me and for yourself?" I'll never forget that. I told him, "Nothing would be more gratifying to me than to be able to come to you in three or four years and say, 'Commissioner, I made you a promise in August of 2009 that I would do everything I possibly could to be the best ambassador on the field and off, and to make you proud of me.'" So you can see why I was so troubled when the shooting happened and my name was being attached to the incident.

I just wanted Commissioner Goodell to know I was a man of my word and that the guy who sat before him in April 2007 and told him those lies was not the guy who came and sat in front of him in August of 2009.

After the Virginia Beach birthday party incident, I telephoned Coach Dungy. I was so upset, I couldn't carry on a conversation. I thought my career could be over. What made matters worse was that I had become lax and hadn't called him for about a two-month stretch. As soon as he picked up the phone and said, "Hello," all I could do was cry. I couldn't even talk to him because I knew how badly I screwed up. I knew all the people I had let down. I knew he was upset. He probably could barely hear what I was saying; I just told him how sorry I was, and I cried so hard.

He kept saying, "You're going to be fine. You've just got to know what situations you're putting yourself in." I didn't believe it. I had lost all hope; I thought that was it. But Coach Dungy still had faith in me—for some reason—and this was merely one day after the incident. It strengthened our bond. Coach Dungy says he could tell I was sincerely remorseful, and he didn't think anything like that would happen again. In the end, he thought the incident was actually good for me because it helped me realize that I would have to take full responsibility for my decisions.

My biggest mistake was not letting my mom and my fiancée have the party they wanted to have—invitation-only, at a place called Nautica's in Virginia Beach. It was going to be over at 1:00 a.m. because the facility didn't stay open late. Mom and Kijafa were only going to invite people who were close to the family, along with some of my teammates and loved ones.

It felt horrible to face my mother about the issue because it troubled her so much. Kijafa scolded me for not putting my foot down and for making decisions like letting Marcus plan the party.

Marcus and I still communicate and talk on the phone, and he'll come down to visit. But I can't go out with him unless it's a stable environment—whether it's at home or at my mom's house.

It hurts because I want to help Marcus, but he seems to resist advice. His NFL career with the Miami Dolphins was very short-lived because of it.

I look at Marcus's life and all the potential he had, and recall everything I ever told him, and I can see he is basically going to do what he wants to do. As close as we are—and everyone knows Marcus and I are airtight—Marcus just won't take the advice that I give him. He's always been that way. He won't come and talk to me if he's having a problem or if he's struggling. But it's different with non-serious things; we'll laugh and joke all day.

Determined that the incident at the birthday party would be the last of its kind, I intensified my commitment to rebuild my reputation.

After a while, it gets old. When you're a grown man, you get tired of having your name in the press for reasons that could have been prevented.

⌒

I entered the 2010 offseason unsure of whether I would remain with the Eagles, even though I had a year remaining on my contract after the team activated that option in early March.

I really thought I was going to be traded. They still had Kevin Kolb and Donovan McNabb. I was just preparing myself and praying that I would end up with another team. News reports said any one of us could be dealt away. Donovan was the longtime starter, and Kevin had been viewed as the starter-in-waiting. I thought I might be the odd man out. But we didn't know for sure. It got to a point where I really wasn't concerned, because my agent assured me I would have the chance to play somewhere. Knowing that gave me confidence.

Eventually, Donovan was traded to the Washington Redskins. I was surprised because they're one of the Eagles' rivals in the NFC East division. It is extremely rare for a player, especially a star, to be traded within a division.

I was also confused. If anyone was going to get traded, it should've been me. I was the No. 3 guy. I hardly played in 2009. I wasn't close enough to Coach Reid at the time to figure out why Donovan was traded. All I could do was worry about myself. The only reason I came up with was that the coaches saw my development in practice—which is true, I was making strides. If the award existed, I probably could have been Scout Team Player of the Week every week. But still, it should have been me who was traded.

With Donovan gone—though I didn't understand it—I was one step closer to getting where I wanted to be. Still, I knew it was Kevin's team. I was going to play the backup role in 2010, and I was fine with that. That was my role. I was content.

⌣

The 2010 offseason was an enjoyable time in my life. It was my first full offseason since coming home, and I had a lot of free time to relax and get my thoughts together about what I was going to do.

I also really had a chance to go out and prepare for the 2010 season. That was a blessing in itself. I had never worked so hard before in any offseason to get ready to play football. I spent time training in Virginia Beach with Tom Anderson, an assistant football and track coach at Landstown High. (We were introduced to one another by my former high school coach Tommy Reamon, who had moved on to become Landstown's head football coach.) This was important because it had taken me much of the 2009 season to get back into shape after nearly two years in prison.

I began working out with Coach Anderson in mid-February, and he put me through a rigid regimen. He worked me hard and wasn't afraid to step up and say, "Mike, this is the way we're going to do things." Coach Anderson wasn't hesitant or timid just because I was Mike Vick. He approached it with a professional attitude and a tough work ethic, like, *We're going to get it done, and we're going to bring you back so you can reap all the benefits we know you are capable of reaping.*

I regained my leg strength and speed working with Coach Anderson. Then I reported to the Eagles' offseason conditioning program. Team strength and conditioning coordinator Barry Rubin picked up where Coach Anderson left off and just took me to a totally different level. I explained to him what I was trying to do—where I wanted to be—and he took over.

This was a whole new way for me. The personal commitment I put into offseason conditioning far exceeded anything I had done when I was with the Falcons. I had never put in that type of time and had never put in that type of work—but now it was paying off. It was great. Before prison, I didn't have that type of work ethic in the NFL. After prison, I wasn't even sure I would have the opportunity to play in the NFL. And now, I had both: work ethic and an opportunity.

I entered the 2010 season refreshed. Strangely, having three years off rejuvenated me.

Even with all the rest I had, I didn't profess to be as fast as I was in my younger days. When I was twenty-two, I could really run, but I never really had long speed. If you think about all my runs, they were just bursts of speed to get out in front.

Though I wasn't twenty-two anymore, I still thought I could run the forty-yard dash in less than 4.5 seconds, which is much faster than other quarterbacks. Age is a big deal, though. You can't outrun Father Time.

The other thing about not playing for three years was that my body hadn't taken the pounding that other thirty-year-old football players' bodies had. I was only twenty-six when I played my last game with the Falcons. Then there were the two years in prison. Then I basically spent a year on the sidelines in 2009. I also played sparingly my rookie year when I was twenty-one, and when I was twenty-three, I didn't play a full season because of an injury. So, I really only had four seasons of wear and tear on my body coming into 2010.

I was glad to stay in Philadelphia. Living there was inspiring in a lot of ways. For example, one of my favorite movie characters, Rocky Balboa, is an icon there. The *Rocky* film series was set in Philly.

I watch *Rocky* every time it's on TV. I could watch that and the movie *Jaws* over and over and over again. *Rocky* exemplifies everything you want in your son, in your father, in yourself—which is strength and courage and a great woman by your side who is very supportive and urges you to do the right things in certain situations. He is just a warrior.

All the *Rocky* movies are inspirational, but especially *Rocky IV*, when he goes to Russia and has to fight Drago. He did it because he believed in himself. That was the only reason. There was no one who could convince him otherwise. It was in his heart.

It's not just the story, though; the music from those movies motivates me too. I remember when I played with Patrick Kerney in Atlanta, he had the *Rocky* soundtrack, and I always asked him if I could borrow his iPod so I could listen to it. The soundtrack is very inspirational.

To many people, the season I would have in 2010 would be very inspirational as well.

Chapter Thirteen

MV 2.0:
The 2010–11 Season

"I've never seen anything like this!"
   —Mike Tirico, ESPN play-by-play announcer

J ust hours before we kicked off our season on September 12 against Green Bay, my high school coach and mentor, Tommy Reamon, told me something profound: "Something is going to happen in this game, and your life is going to change forever."

Right, I thought to myself. *What are you talking about? I'm the backup quarterback. I'm No. 2. Whatcha think is going to happen? Think I'm going to score three touchdowns from the shotgun running a quarterback draw?*

As expected, Kevin Kolb entered the season and the game as our starting quarterback. Honestly, I figured it would stay that way the whole season. I thought Kevin would thrive and do well. And as I said, I was back in the NFL—that was a start—and I was content.

Kevin, however, sustained a concussion on a hard hit by Packers linebacker Clay Matthews at the end of the first half and was sidelined. I never want to see someone get hurt—especially a teammate—no matter what position he plays and no matter what position I'm fighting for. I remember seeing Kevin on the ground, hoping and praying he'd go back into the game. I wasn't prepared. The only package I had was the Wildcat. I had studied throughout the week, but I hadn't studied thoroughly to the point of knowing the ins and outs of every concept. I was nervous because I didn't want to go out and embarrass myself.

In the locker room at halftime, I remember one of my teammates—I think it was Juqua Parker—coming up to me. "The door has been opened for you," he said. "Whatcha gonna do? You gonna go through it or walk away from it?"

Each and every play that game, I wasn't trying to prove that I was back; I was just trying to win. I knew I had a shot to show everyone that I could still play the game. But I knew it was Kevin's team. More than anything, I was trying to show the Philadelphia coaches, potential teams, and football fans that I could still play. Remember, I didn't have a contract. I was auditioning for a potential job around the league.

We were down 20-3 that game, but we nearly pulled off a comeback win, losing to the eventual Super Bowl champions 27-20. I threw for 175 yards and a touchdown and ran for 103 yards on 11 carries.

I remember looking over at the Green Bay bench as I walked off the field that game. *One more half,* I said to myself. *One more half, and we would've destroyed you guys.*

After the game, I talked to Coach Reamon again, and he said, "I told you."

The way he prophesied that—I couldn't put it all together. I still don't know what to think of it. But when he told me that before the game, I could hear it in his voice. He wasn't just saying it. He was extremely adamant and passionate about what he was saying.

He was right.

⁓

Because Kevin wasn't cleared by team doctors, he was also sidelined the following week against Detroit. And for the first time since my prison sentence—for the first time since the 2006 season—I was starting.

We were going up against the Detroit Lions. They had a tough defense, so I knew it would be a challenge, but I was excited because I had more time to prepare and had been studying all week.

Still, my mindset had nothing to do with making an epic return to the NFL. We were 0-1 after our loss to Green Bay, so I kept telling myself, *We gotta win. We gotta win.* It was all I was thinking. On a personal level, I knew this was still Kevin's team; but if I played well, I might have a chance to earn a contract on another team. First and foremost, I needed to get the Eagles a victory.

Going into the game, however, was also bittersweet, because before every game I started in Atlanta, I had called my grandmother. I liked to check up on her and see how she was doing; and talking to someone I loved help take the pressure off me and put the game in its proper perspective. She calmed my nerves and helped me kick the butterflies.

Now, I didn't have that. She was gone. To this day, nobody plays that role, although before the Detroit game, I did call my pastor and we talked.

I cried in my room. It was sad that I couldn't share the moment with my grandmother.

I wish she could have seen that game. We beat Detroit 35-32, and I passed for 280-some yards. I did my job. As a backup quarterback, I helped get us the win, and improve our record to 1-1 for Kevin to take over the team for the remainder of the season.

⌒

I was on stage, and my phone kept vibrating in my pocket.

C'mon, I was thinking to myself. *Is it* that *serious?*

The week following our victory against Detroit, I was speaking to youth at a "What It Takes" event about the mistakes I'd made and the importance of making good choices. But my phone kept vibrating—over and over.

When I checked my phone, I had a text from Coach Reid saying, "Call me ASAP."

I knew exactly what it was about. I knew he'd either tell me "You'll start this week," or "Kevin isn't ready yet."

I called Coach Reid.

He always starts phone conversations with a quick, "How ya doing?"

"Good," I said.

Then there was a long, awkward pause.

"Look here," he said, dragging the conversation out a little. "I'm gonna make you the starter."

Coach Reid initially had said Kevin would remain the starter once he returned from injury, but then he changed his mind and named me the permanent starter.

I was amazed by the sudden change in my status. I was caught off guard because I had gotten so relaxed at being a backup that I started feeling like a backup.

I knew what it was like to be a starter in this league. I knew the pressure—what it takes and how much it can take out of you. And just like that—*boom*—I was back in that position. I was thinking, *Hold on, I didn't prepare for this. I'm not ready.*

At Virginia Tech, I remember looking on that depth chart and seeing "Vick—No. 1." I remember how proud I felt that I had fought and beat out Dave Meyer for the starting role. Being named the starter at Philly, however, was completely different.

There wasn't a competition between Kevin and me, because I had accepted the backup role. Philadelphia was his team. And I could live with that.

Right when I hung up the phone, I knew I had to get my mind right. I called my counselor, who I met with regularly through the NFL.

"Man, we gotta talk," he said after I gave him the news.

In order to perform week in and week out and be consistent, I had to approach each game correctly from a mental standpoint. I was excited. But I was also nervous. This was something I didn't expect. It's tough to play in Philly, and it's easy to get booed on

Sunday. Who wants to get booed with your family in the stands? I sure didn't. All the ability in the world means nothing if you can't *think* and play. I needed to sharpen my mind.

It was hard to wrap my mind around everything that was happening. It was happening so fast. Sitting in a cell in Leavenworth, I never doubted that I'd play in the NFL again. I knew I would get there, and I knew I could start at some point. I just couldn't put a time frame on it.

The only thing I could go back to was that this was all God's plan. There was a reason behind it, so I was going to enjoy it, because I knew He was with me every step of the way.

Things became even more unbelievable as the season wore on.

We beat Jacksonville 28-3 in Week 3. I was motivated before the game by our chapel service. The speaker talked about how Jesus made the great sacrifice of dying on the cross for our sins. I had already asked Jesus to forgive my sins and be the Lord of my life, but I was sitting there thinking, *Man, all this for us? Why can't I sacrifice for Him?* I made a promise that day and thought to myself, *I'm going to sacrifice for Him and try to do the right things on a day-to-day basis.* Then I went out, and the Lord blessed me with a good game. I threw three touchdown passes and ran for another.

A few days later, my friend Arthur Blank—the owner of the Falcons—called to congratulate me and to talk, which meant a lot to me.

I was shocked that Mr. Blank called; but at the same time, I wasn't. We'd had a great relationship in Atlanta; I just didn't take advantage of everything he had to offer. He wanted nothing but the best for me, and he probably would have liked to play the role of a mentor in my life. But I didn't want to continually come to him with questions and overstep my boundaries. As a man, I felt like I should be able to take care of myself and make my own decisions. But I was twenty-four or twenty-five. I wasn't a man. I was a kid. Knowing what I do now, I would go back and confide in Mr. Blank more, and things would have never ended up the way they did. But it happened.

"Take advantage of the opportunity," he told me on the phone that day. "Don't lose sight of how you got into the position you're in. I'm rooting for you every game until we play you."

Next was a big Redskins-Eagles showdown in Philly. The game had more than enough storylines to make it the national game of the week. It was a homecoming for former Eagles quarterback and my good buddy Donovan McNabb. The McNabb-returns-to-Philly talk was big, and so was a McNabb-versus-Vick theme, since Donovan had played a key role in the Eagles signing me the previous year.

I really wanted to win that game. I hadn't had too much success against Donovan; he and the Eagles beat us twice in the playoffs when I was with Atlanta.

The Redskins got off to a quick start, but we were in the midst of a rally when I suffered fractured ribs on a run near the goal line. I got sandwiched between two Washington defenders, including my former Atlanta teammate and friend, cornerback DeAngelo Hall. I had to leave the game, and the Redskins went on to win, 17-12.

I would miss three games because of the injury. And as disappointed as I was to miss out on the game against Donovan, I was more disappointed to miss the game against the Falcons. It was a game where Kevin led us to a 31-17 win.

Overall, we were 2-1 during the stretch while I was gone; Kevin did a very nice job. When I was healthy, Coach Reid put me back under center. I was still the starter.

⌇

I returned to the lineup for a November 7 matchup against Indianapolis, which was quarterbacked by Peyton Manning.

The Colts always seemed to be one of the best teams, so it was a huge confidence builder for us that we won 26-24. I threw one touchdown and ran for another.

It was great to have an opportunity to get out and play the game you love so dearly against some of the best competition. Going up against Peyton, I knew it was going to be a tough challenge, and I knew it would be a game that went down to the wire. We would have to do everything right.

We just put it all together against the Colts. And our locker room was absolutely crazy. Winning that game felt like we had won the Super Bowl.

The celebration was unique for a regular season game. Cornerback Asante Samuel and wide receiver DeSean Jackson were our primary cheerleaders.

Anytime you're in a locker room after a win, it's a dynamic atmosphere. It's also a moment you have to cherish because you don't get it that often. You have sixteen games minimum; it's unlikely that you'll win them all. The feeling only lasts for about thirty minutes, and then it's over as far as being with the guys. But some wins are more special than others.

After that game, I remember telling myself for the first time, *I'm back. I'm back to being the player I know I can be.*

⌒⌒

The next week—a November 15 *Monday Night Football* game at Washington—was when we got a second chance at Donovan and the Redskins. The pregame hype was intense.

Some of what will follow here is almost embarrassing for me to include, but my coauthors, publisher, and I believe we need to do so in order to best characterize the season and to make sure things are presented fully and accurately. One of the main reasons this is important is because God did amazing things in my life and career through the course of the season, and I want to make absolutely certain He is glorified. So please know that it is with humility and a desire for God to get the credit that I present these things to you.

Going into that Monday night game against the Redskins, I already had been named NFC Offensive Player of the Month for September and Offensive Player of the Week in early November. Even before kickoff, the ESPN announcers were raving on the telecast about my play up to that point. Steve Young, Ron Jaworski, and Jon Gruden all said I'd been playing better than ever.

Young is the former San Francisco 49ers star that I grew up

emulating. Jaworski formerly starred at quarterback for Philadelphia, and Gruden coached at Oakland and Tampa Bay, winning a Super Bowl with the Buccaneers.

Young said on the pregame show: "Personally, this is the Michael Vick I dreamed of seeing when he came out of college. I used to talk to him and [say], 'Look, if you can learn to throw the football from the pocket, and also use your legs outside the pocket when it's time—if you can actually learn the quarterback job—you can be the greatest weapon at quarterback there has ever been in the NFL.'" It was big talk and seemed to border on excessive hype—but then the game started, and we got off to a roaring start.

On the first play, I threw an 88-yard touchdown pass to DeSean Jackson. It was the longest gain on an opening play in team history. I scored on a 7-yard run on our second possession, and we were ahead 28-0 after the first quarter—the biggest lead a road team has had after one quarter in NFL history.

ESPN play-by-play announcer Mike Tirico exulted: "I've never seen anything like this!" Gruden added, "This is just an unbelievable start by Michael Vick."

Next up, I tossed a 48-yard touchdown pass to Jeremy Maclin on the first play of the second quarter to increase the lead to 35-0. Gruden would later say, "Mike could be the NFL Player of the Year right now. He could be the Player of the Decade."

It is with gratitude to God, my coaches, and my teammates that I can tell you I became the first quarterback in NFL history to pass for more than 300 yards (333) and four touchdowns, plus rush for more than 50 yards (80) and two touchdowns on the ground in a single game. We had a runaway win that night, beating the Redskins 59-28.

By the end of the game, the Pro Football Hall of Fame was prompted to call, asking for the jersey I wore to be sent in for display in its Canton, Ohio, gallery.

Former NFL quarterback Trent Dilfer said on ESPN's postgame show: "I don't know what to say about the transformation of Michael Vick. I haven't seen anything like this. There is a little bit of a panic mode setting in around the National Football League."

Young added: "There are not enough words. Truly, you're seeing something extraordinary here. This was what we talked about when he came out of college. It is what we thought was possible. It is so exciting to me. This performance shows you that at the position of quarterback, you can crush teams. [Michael] was unstoppable. You can talk about this in any superlative you want. This was one of the [best] games at quarterback I have ever seen."

Gruden kiddingly gave me the nickname "Starship Seven," a take on my jersey number. "Where he is now is a totally different place than Michael Vick has ever been," he said.

Young predicted the performance would be my signature game: "This game will always be known as when Michael Vick was not just a highlight film, but actually dictated what happened in a football game."

I tried to downplay all the fuss over my performance, but I must say that I've never had a game where I had so many stats.

Everything was clicking on all cylinders for the entire team. The offensive line, running backs, and receivers all played great. You dream about having a game like that.

Yet I believed I could play even better.

You know how much Coach Dungy's opinion means to me, so I was especially humbled when he said he believed I was throwing from the pocket as well as any quarterback in the NFL, including Tom Brady and Peyton Manning. He also said my running ability gave the Eagles a talent equivalent to Chicago's Devin Hester in the backfield. Hester is a dynamic wide receiver and record-setting kick returner, so I consider that a tremendous compliment.

"You can't play certain defenses against him," Coach Dungy said of me. He also said my style of play most resembled two of my favorites—Steve Young and Randall Cunningham.

Interestingly, the 80 yards I gained on the ground against the Redskins made me the No. 2 rusher among quarterbacks in NFL history, surpassing Young. By the time the season was over, I had 4,630 career rushing yards. Now, I have more rushing yards than any other quarterback in NFL history.

One of the things I feel best about regarding the 2010 season is that I put in the extra time like I never did in Atlanta. I spent significant parts of Tuesdays—the players' regular weekly day off—at the stadium, preparing for the upcoming game. Unlike my time with the Falcons, I tried to arrive early and stay late throughout the week.

I'm taking the game more seriously now. I realize I may only have five or six more good years left in me before I have to take a backup role somewhere or face possible retirement. The extra work has made a tremendous difference in my play.

I'm also evolving as a player as I get older. I know I can't run around as much as I used to. So it's good that in the offense I'm in now—the West Coast offense—there are opportunities to get the ball out quickly. There are more options, and there's a lot of young talent around me—guys like DeSean Jackson, Jeremy Maclin, our running back LeSean McCoy, and our tight end Brent Celek. Those guys are amazing! So instead of using my legs all the time, I only use them when I need to. As time goes on, I think I'll run even less. But I'll still run when I have to.

It's been said that I can't be a great quarterback without using my legs a lot. It's one of the reasons I play the game—to prove those people wrong, to prove to all the naysayers who claim I can't throw the football or that a quarterback with my type of abilities will never win a Super Bowl, that they are wrong.

One of the big benefits for me here in Philly is that I'm extremely blessed to have some of the best, most experienced offensive coaches in the game in Andy Reid and Marty Mornhinweg, our offensive coordinator. They've coached quarterbacks like Brett Favre and my idol, Steve Young.

Even the backups who have played for Coach Reid and Coach Mornhinweg have played well when called upon. It just goes to show that the system they run is great, and they do an excellent job of game planning.

They've helped me get better in so many ways. Just evolving as a quarterback is probably the biggest thing, making sure I do all the things a quarterback is required to do. Marty is always talking about Steve. He'll say, "When I had Steve Young, we used to do it this way." I was humbled after the season to see Marty quoted as saying he thought I had a chance to be even better than Steve.

The *Monday Night Football* performance against the Redskins seemed to further launch our team and me into the national consciousness. Suddenly, there were moral issues being debated: Did my play trump the past mistakes I'd made? Did I deserve to be forgiven? The issues would remain in the media for the rest of the season.

NFL commissioner Roger Goodell, the man who suspended and reinstated me, was among many to step forward with support. He did so immediately after the Redskins game. "There is a big message in what Michael is doing," the commissioner told the *New York Daily News*. "He's a superstar athlete who everyone thought had everything in the world. He fell from grace tragically by making some horrific mistakes, paid a significant price, worked his way back in and now he's being successful. It demonstrates to me [the need] to get to these young men earlier and work with them and make them understand their responsibility, making decisions that will define them for a period of time."

"There are so many examples in our society of failure, people falling short," Goodell added. "We need more success stories. I'm hoping Michael Vick will be a success story. People need to see that. People need to be inspired by that—a person made a tragic error and he's overcome it."

Those words meant a lot because I have such a special relationship with Commissioner Goodell and I'm committed to making him proud of me. He has become a bit of a father figure, friend, and mentor. During the season, we were talking or texting at least once a week. I can pick up the phone and call him anytime I'm having a problem. He has continued to advise me on having good people around me and making sure I'm making rational decisions on a day-to-day basis because I'm being watched each and every day. There are people out there who don't want to see me excel. They want to see me fail.

A flurry of articles ensued, delving into my background and the topic of forgiveness, like the one in *Sports Illustrated* that asked whether or not it was okay to cheer for me. Or the one in the *New York Times* quoting John Lord, a professor and chairman of the marketing department at Philadelphia's St. Joseph's University, who reasoned that it was okay "to forgive and forget because that seems to be where the momentum is going."

Writers who covered me—and some who didn't—began to explore questions usually reserved for pastors and philosophers. Sam Donnellon, a columnist for the *Philadelphia Daily News*, agreed that it was okay for people to get second chances, but he questioned whether or not it was too soon for that to happen in my case.

It had been more than three years since I had been convicted and sent to prison, but people still wondered if it had been long enough. The season before, when I was sitting on the bench, not much was being said or written. But once I began having success, people began weighing in.

⌒

Through nine games, we were 6-3—tied for first with the New York Giants in the NFC East Division.

The next game, on November 21, was huge—at home against the Giants. With seven games remaining, and two of those against each other, playoff positioning and winning the division were foremost on our minds.

We beat the Giants 27-17 to take sole possession of first place in the division with a 7-3 record.

Increasingly in interviews, I was getting asked more about life than football. After a game, a reporter asked me if I was at peace because everything was going well for me. I said I was at peace the season before, even when I was on the bench, and that I was just happy to be playing football.

I doubt that's the answer he expected.

One thing I've noticed is that reporters are going to be reporters. Their job is to make a story sound good or to make a story sound extremely bad. You just have to anticipate both good and bad questions and know how you're going to respond.

⌒

Judges generally don't talk about football players, but the 2010 season was an exception. Much to my amazement, the man who sentenced me in 2007 spoke out publicly to compliment me.

In early December, the *Washington Post* was working on a story about the legal challenges to the health-care law and interviewed Judge Henry Hudson, who was hearing the case. While they were asking him about that, they also asked him about my on-field success and off-field progress. "He's an example of how the system can work," Judge Hudson said of me. "He's having a terrific season. I'm very happy for him. I wish him the best of success."

It meant a lot coming from him.

He made a decision in my life that was pivotal, at a time in my life when nothing really mattered to me. He was probably the only one who thought that a twenty-three-month prison sentence was what I needed to get my life turned around. To see what he said in the paper was gratifying since it demonstrated that I was changing the minds of people who once felt differently about me. It definitely showed me that I was on the right track and doing the right things.

When I first got sentenced, I felt like it was a harsh punishment, but I also had to think about the things that transpired during my pretrial release period. I wasn't respectful to the courts; I wasn't respectful to the public. Judge Hudson knew why he put me in prison for that long, and it's great for him to see me come out and have success, knowing that he did it for a reason. I commend him for that, and I'll continue to make him proud.

It's just the beginning. It won't stop here. I'll have to continue to make great strides.

Judge Hudson was the first of several high-profile people who would comment on how a second chance had helped me and what they thought about it. In between, though, I was still playing football and trying to help the Eagles secure a playoff berth and, hopefully, a Super Bowl title.

⌒

After a win over Dallas, we had another signature game.

On December 19, at the Giants' new stadium in East Rutherford, New Jersey (the Meadowlands), we trailed 31-10 with seven and a half minutes remaining, and came from behind to win 38-31. Like any other game, we went into that one thinking we were going to win, but obviously, when you fall that far behind, there is a sense of doubt and you start thinking ahead to next week.

I'll never forget that game, though. DeSean Jackson and I were on the sidelines talking, and he was kind of discouraged. I encouraged him to stay in the game and stay focused and keep fighting. I told him that, regardless of anything else that happened, we were going to leave there with some pride and some dignity about ourselves and be able to say we gave it everything we had. Right after that, we scored a touchdown on our next possession. Then a second and a third and a fourth followed and, before you knew it, we had won the game.

DeSean came up with the game-winning punt return for a touchdown as time expired. It was like a walk-off grand slam home run to win the game. It was amazing! I just couldn't believe it happened the way it did.

I was blessed to throw three touchdown passes in the game, and to run for 130 yards and another score. Fox TV announcer Jimmy Johnson was among those who felt I was a leading candidate for the MVP award, which eventually—and deservedly—went to Tom Brady.

The win over the Giants essentially clinched the NFC East for us. It was called a "comeback for the ages" and was dubbed "the New Miracle at the New Meadowlands." At the old Giants Stadium, the Eagles had beaten the Giants 19-17 in November 1978, in a game called simply "the Miracle at the Meadowlands." In that one, Philadelphia scored a touchdown on a bizarre fumble return to win. This win seemed just as unlikely as that one.

We were 10-4; we owned the tiebreaker for the division title over the Giants because we had won both games against them; and things seemed good.

⌒

Just before our next game, a report by *Sports Illustrated* writer and NBC broadcaster Peter King opened up a firestorm. King reported that President Barack Obama had called Eagles owner Jeffrey Lurie to discuss alternative energy that he was pushing for at Lincoln Financial Field, and my name came up in the conversation.

Mr. Lurie told King: "The president said, 'So many people who serve time never get a fair second chance.' He was passionate about it. He said it's never a level playing field for prisoners when they get out of jail. And he was happy that we did something on such a national stage that showed our faith in giving someone a second chance after such a major downfall."

I was just ecstatic when I heard that. After all, it's the president of the United States, and it doesn't get any better than that. I was very surprised he would mention my name.

I was so grateful to have such a prominent person commend me in front of the entire world about everything that I had worked for and tried to accomplish. It kind of showed that I was on the right track and I was doing the right thing. I hope those comments reverberated around the world to people who are trying to make a comeback and have been given a second chance—to those who are trying to do things right the second time around.

A lot of people don't get that opportunity. I was one of the ones who did, and I'm thankful and blessed. For those comments to come from President Obama was big. For a lot of kids who come from broken families, or who may not be as confident or as fortunate as others, those comments will convince them to strive harder in what they're trying to do in life. If they feel they're not making progress, or if they have been in some trouble and they're trying to climb out of the hole they dug for themselves, knowing that someone believes they're able to do it gives them a sense of hope.

Though the phone conversation really didn't have anything to do with me, I think the statement shows how strongly the president feels about people getting second chances. Obviously he does, or he wouldn't have said it.

President Obama's comments didn't sit well with everyone, though. The whole issue became very political and polarizing. Feedback from a wide range of commentators—conservative and liberal—showed that people thought prison, bankruptcy, and more than three years of being removed from a bad situation wasn't enough.

The most prominent critic was Fox News commentator Tucker Carlson, who was hosting a panel on December 28, 2010, the same night we played the Minnesota Vikings. He was filling in for conservative talk-show host Sean Hannity. Carlson said I should have been "executed" for what I did to dogs.

Carlson said he was a Christian, that he had made mistakes, and that he fervently believes in second chances—but not in my case. "Michael Vick killed dogs, and he did it in a heartless and cruel way," Carlson said on the air. "I think, personally, he should've been executed for that. . . . The idea that the president of the United States would be getting behind someone who murdered dogs [is] kind of beyond the pale."

"I'm all for forgiveness," Carlson continued. "[But] I think there are some things that are unforgivable, and Michael Vick did one of those things in hurting dogs. However, why is the president weighing in on this?"

The fact that Carlson would make such an emotionally charged statement showed the depths to which the subject had affected people.

Carlson didn't have everyone's support. Doug Schoen, a Fox News contributor on the show, felt differently.

"Bottom line, he did a horrific thing," Schoen said. "He paid; he went to jail; he is speaking for the Humane Society . . . he has turned his life around. The Humane Society has said even Michael Vick may well be able to have a dog at some point in the future, and the president acknowledged that this is a country of second chances with a high-profile felon who has acknowledged his foibles. And, you know what? The president was right to make this point, because it's a metaphor, Tucker."

After being interrupted, Schoen said, "This is about redemption, not a policy decision you don't like. . . . At Christmas[time], to talk about redemption is not the worst thing in the world, Tucker."

I stayed out of the whole issue and didn't respond. But I can tell you now that I was stunned by what Carlson said. When I first heard it, I was like, *Wow!* I mean, wishing death on another person? I think for me not to respond at the time was the best decision, because it's foolish and irrelevant when someone says things like that. But the statement put me in the position to do what I've been talking about—to forgive someone.

I forgave him when he said it, but some people won't forgive you when they feel like you've done something wrong. Everybody's heart isn't the same; everybody doesn't think alike. Some people forgive, some people don't. I think people let their emotions get the best of them in situations, and their true inner feelings may show.

After a huge backlash, Tucker later apologized and said he got "too emotional" and that he "overspoke." He said he was "uncomfortable with the death penalty in any circumstance. Of course I don't think [Michael Vick] should be executed." I appreciated that.

One of the things that really blessed me was receiving support from People for the Ethical Treatment of Animals (PETA). Previously, PETA had not shown the same support for me that the Humane Society of the United States demonstrated. Ingrid E. Newkirk, the president of PETA, told *Washington Post* reporter Perry Bacon Jr. that Obama's comments concerning my getting a second chance after spending time in prison were "appropriate."

"Obama's a sports guy, Vick's a sports guy, and comebacks and redemption can happen," Newkirk told Bacon. "We all want a president who can lift us up and move us forward when ugly things happen, but that cannot let us forget . . . [we must] remain watchful to avoid future abuses."

⌒

While all of this was going on, my teammates and I focused on the two games we had remaining. A major winter storm caused our Sunday night, December 26, home game against Minnesota to be delayed by two days. It caused quite a controversy in Philadelphia, where fans are accustomed to attending games in extremely inclement weather.

We scored first against the Vikings but went on to lose 24-14. Nevertheless, we clinched the division championship and were locked in as the No. 3 seed in the NFC. Several starters, including me, were held out of the final game of the season on January 2 at home against Dallas, mainly because we couldn't improve our playoff seed. It was done as a safety precaution and also to give us time to rest up for the postseason. Dallas won 14-13 on a touchdown with less than a minute remaining, and we finished the regular season 10-6.

Our goal all along had been to reach and win the Super Bowl, so we excitedly approached the start of the playoffs. But our dream season ended when the No. 6-seeded Green Bay Packers, who would go on to win the Super Bowl, beat us 21-16 at Lincoln Financial Field. It was our third consecutive loss at home, which is tough to even think about now.

I passed for 292 yards and a touchdown and scored a touchdown on a 1-yard run with 4:02 remaining to bring us to within five points of the Packers. We were driving for a possible come-from-behind win, but I was intercepted in the end zone with forty-four seconds left.

It was very disappointing not to advance in the playoffs, but the further away we get from that game, the more we'll appreciate the fact that we had a really good season. Our season began and ended with losses to the eventual Super Bowl championship team, and a lot of exciting things happened in between—things that gave us a lot to build on as we look ahead to the future.

Our offense ranked third in the league in scoring with 439 points. And I finished 2010 with the best season of my career.

God deserves all the glory. I set career highs in passing yards (3,018), touchdown passes (21), rushing touchdowns (9), completion percentage (62.6), and passer rating (100.2). It was the first time I had thrown for more than 3,000 yards in a season, and it happened despite playing, basically, eleven games. I missed three games with injuries, was held out of the season finale to rest, didn't play most of the first half in the season opener until Kevin Kolb was injured, and didn't play in the second half of our first game against Washington because of injured ribs. When you put it all together, that's about eleven games for me.

～～

One of the ways I was encouraged and supported by the fans was through the Pro Bowl balloting, which ended the day after we beat the Giants. Given everything I'd been through, I truly experienced grace in how they voted for me. I wound up second in the league in votes and was the top NFC player.

Tom Brady had 1,877,079 votes to my 1,522,437. It meant a lot that fans were able to overlook my past and focus on the present. I wanted to perform well for them because they had been behind me during some trying times. I also wanted to prove to others that I could still play at a high level even after being gone from the game for so long.

I think the fans respect what I've been through and how I've come back from it. I missed some of the best years of my football life: from the ages of twenty-seven to twenty-nine, I didn't play. I missed the game. When I returned, I was more motivated so that I could be in the top echelon and be a part of that great group with Tom Brady, Peyton Manning, Drew Brees, and Aaron Rodgers. You know, there are a lot of great quarterbacks in the league, and I feel I'm one of the best, and I just wanted to show it.

It was good going back to the Pro Bowl for the fourth time. It was really cool that the man who replaced me as the Falcons quarterback, Matt Ryan, was there, and that the Atlanta coaches were the coaches for the NFC team.

~~

I had hoped to be busily working with the Eagles during Super Bowl week in the Dallas area, but our efforts fell short. However, I still went to Texas to be involved in many events during the week. And though I had stayed clear of any trouble during the season, some seemed to find me in Dallas.

Several pre-Super Bowl parties used my name without my permission. Roger Goodell and others didn't want me involved in the party scene surrounding the game, and I assured them that I wouldn't be. This was a situation I needed to clear up, and I did. It was a chance to show consistency of character, and I was proud to be above reproach in that situation. Like I said, I was in Dallas for more important things.

While there, I had the opportunity to speak to teenagers at an area school. As always, it felt good to share my story with them, and hopefully I provided some hope and inspiration. When the event was over, a Dallas radio reporter, Richard Hunter of KFXR-AM 1190, tried to talk to me as security was ushering me away. Hunter said he had adopted one of my former dogs and he wanted to show me a picture of it and ask how I felt about the matter. Some media outlets called Hunter's attempt at an unscheduled interview an "ambush" and said that Hunter "harassed" me and "crossed the line" since the security people with me repeatedly told him that we had to leave. Angered that he didn't get the interview, Hunter released a video with written commentary regarding the incident. He seemed upset that I didn't give him the time he apparently wanted.

I understood the situation: He adopted one of the dogs. Here was a guy who cared. He was very fortunate because, obviously, he got a good dog and gave him a home. Now he has one of man's best friends, and he should be happy about that. I am not really sure what he expected or wanted from me. I know I didn't brush him off, though. I told him it was a good thing he did, and I kept going.

The criticism I took for my past wasn't limited to media members. During the beginning of Major League Baseball's spring training in February, Chicago White Sox pitcher Mark Buehrle jumped in the fray. Buehrle, known for pitching a no-hitter in 2007 and a perfect game in 2009, said he and his wife were dog lovers, and that while they watched NFL games in 2010, they were hoping I'd get injured. When given the chance to retract the statements, he didn't back down.

I feel bad for people like that because they're so worried about me. You know, I don't even know who the guy is. If Buehrle walked right past me in the local 7-Eleven, I wouldn't know it was him. But for him to make that type of comment, it's something he has to live with. Don't wish bad things on others.

⌒

In the midst of all this controversy, I was awarded the NFL Comeback Player of the Year and the Bert Bell Award, an award that was established in 1959 and is given by the Maxwell Football Club in recognition of the best professional football player in America each year. Both awards were humbling, and I felt extremely honored to be esteemed in such a way. In some respect, it was evidence and proof of what hard work and being committed to the proper priorities can help someone achieve.

The Eagles recognized that too, and they chose to put their franchise tag on me during the initial free-agency period. It meant I would get paid a 2011 salary at the average of the five highest-paid quarterbacks in 2010—about $20 million, a significant raise from the $5.2 million salary I had made in 2010. It was a lot of money, but I still have millions to repay to creditors as part of my bankruptcy settlement.

In the fall of 2011 I signed a new long-term contract, a five-year, $80 million deal with $35.5 million guaranteed. One of my friends called me afterward. "Boy, you better say a prayer," he said. "God really loves you. There's something about you."

I never imagined making that type of money again. Sitting in prison, I knew I'd play again. But financially, I didn't think I'd ever see money like that. I figured I'd have a couple of one-year deals and maybe a three-year deal but never imagined making $80 million. I just wanted to earn enough to pay off my creditors and support my family for the rest of our lives.

At the press conference for my contract, I was just humbled to be a part of the Eagles organization. They will forever hold a dear place in my heart because of the opportunity they gave me. Words can't explain how I feel about them. They believed in me, took a chance on me—and I was determined to give back to them. Ultimately, I knew it came from God—putting me in Philly, placing me around great coaches who care about me on and off the field.

In the first couple of months after the season ended, I received my first paid endorsements since getting out of prison. The first came in February and was a two-year deal with Unequal Technologies, which supplied me with a vest, shoulder pads, and thigh pads during the season. Later, in March, I signed a deal with Core Synergy to endorse titanium-based wristbands, which help hold a positive charge and can reverse pain in the body caused by negative energy fields. Then, in July, I signed again with Nike, the sports apparel company that had cut ties with me about four years earlier. The same month, I also signed with MusclePharm, a nutritional supplement company.

In April, I was a finalist, along with Cleveland Browns running back Peyton Hillis, to be on the cover of the EA Sports *Madden NFL '12* video game. Peyton ended up winning. If I had won, I would have become the first player to appear on the cover twice. Instead, Peyton became the first Cleveland Browns player on the cover. It was special to see Peyton accept the honor and thank the fans for voting for him when he announced his team's first-round pick during the 2011 NFL draft.

I was so happy for the fan vote too. Even though I didn't win, it let me know that there are fans who are standing behind me and who believe in me. Things happen for a reason, and if I'm not on the cover, it's for a reason. I never question what God has in store for my life.

Around that same time, another game—*Dog Wars* by Kage Games—was released. Designed to run on Google Inc.'s Android software, it glorified dogfighting. I tried to be proactive and immediately issued a statement opposing it. The statement, released on the Humane Society's website, said: "I've come to learn the hard way that dogfighting is a dead-end street. Now I am on the right side of this issue, and I think it's important to send the smart message to kids, and not glorify this form of animal cruelty, even in an Android app."

It was another step on my journey toward healing and redemption. I now look ahead to all that God has in store for my life.

Chapter Fourteen
Moving Forward

"My comeback is far from over."

I'm so excited about the future.

I know some people may never forgive me, but I also know that I have asked for and received forgiveness from God. That, combined with the love of family and friends, helps me continue to try to live out the promises I've made and my commitment to taking full advantage of the second chance I've been given.

I'm trying to do all the right things: I'm trying to be a model citizen. I'm trying to be responsible, to be an ambassador, to be a great father. I want to show the world that I'm not just going to talk the talk; I'm going to walk the walk as well.

I'm doing everything I can to turn a negative into a positive. It's only by the grace of God that I have this opportunity before me. He has allowed me to go out and show the world that when you fall, you can rise again. You can fly again. But you have to be willing to put in the hard work. You have to be humble. You have to be obedient. You have to be willing to hold yourself accountable.

I'd be lying if I said this journey has been easy. The scrutiny and negative talk aren't easy to deal with all the time, but I have to accept it.

I want my life to make a major difference all across the world to a lot of people. I want my trademark and my comeback statement to be: I hit the bottom, but with God's help, I also rose back to the top.

Tony Dungy says that if I stay on the right track, I can have that kind of influence. "As much as I like to go around and spread the gospel," he said in an interview, "as much as I would like to talk to kids about staying in school and doing the right things and how important education is, there is going to be a certain group of kids I could never reach.

"They're going to look at me as an old ex-coach who doesn't really know what they're dealing with. But when Mike Vick talks to them, they know he has walked the same streets and he's been where they are. He's going to impact a generation that I know I never could. I think that is one of the things the Lord is going to do with him."

⌣⌣

I am blessed to speak frequently to youth and school groups, especially in conjunction with the Humane Society. It provides me the chance to discuss the ills of dogfighting and to urge young people to avoid the mistakes I made.

I tell them to use me as an example of what not to do, and to avoid dogfighting at all costs.

Ironically, many of the talks during the football season happen on Tuesdays, my off day and also the day of the week when I used to travel from Atlanta to Virginia to oversee our dogfighting operation.

I try to share my testimony in ways that translate to kids' lives as an example to stay away from all types of danger and to let them know they can accomplish whatever they set out to do. I talk about the severe consequences that resulted from my bad decisions. Just as you work hard to get somewhere in life, or to accomplish certain things, or to have prized personal possessions—having all of that taken away from you after you work so hard for it is a horrible, horrible feeling. That's the case regardless of the magnitude, regardless of the scale you're on or your position in life, whether you're white-collar, blue-collar, or whatever. It can all be taken away from you, and it will hurt.

My partnership with the Humane Society means so much to me. It all started when Wayne Pacelle, who heads that organization, came to see me in prison and let me know he believed in me. Since then, I've spoken at more than thirty Humane Society events around the country. The first one was in Atlanta. I'll never forget how nervous I was that day, but it went well.

It's an honor to be one of their representatives. I appreciate the opportunity to speak against dogfighting and to hopefully change people's perception about pit bulls. Some people think they are the worst dogs in the world, when they actually are among the smartest and friendliest breeds.

I'm happy to say that dogfighting is on the decline. Not as many dogs are fighting and getting hurt. I never heard anyone talk about the evils of dogfighting growing up. I take this platform very seriously, and I want to shed a new light that dogfighting is harmful, inhumane, and unethical.

⌒

I really wanted to see some results from all the talks I had been giving to kids about the dangers of dogfighting, so I asked Chris Shigas, my public relations counsel, what I could do. I wanted to do more than just give my testimony, because I'm only one person and I can only talk to so many people. I wanted to be more of an advocate.

After talking to Chris, we took the idea to Wayne Pacelle, the president of the Humane Society of the United States. Wayne saw a great opportunity for me to come to Capitol Hill and draw attention to some of the inadequate animal welfare laws.

It was July 2011, and I remember walking with Wayne and Chris through the halls of Congress where there was this gorgeous, ornate architecture. I thought, *This is the real deal.* This wasn't some football field anymore. I wanted to make a real difference, and here we were.

Wayne and I gave our support for legislation that would make it a misdemeanor for anyone attending a dogfight or a cockfight. Now it is against the law to conduct one, but not against the law to attend one. And we also gave our support for legislation that would make it a felony to take a child to a dogfight or a cockfight.

As I said earlier, I was eight years old when I saw my first dogfight. Back then, police would come to the dogfights and break them up, but no one would be arrested.

That day in DC was more than Wayne and me voicing support on Capitol Hill for legislation. Our time was spent in private meetings with congressional staff, the black caucus, and other lawmakers. We also held a press conference to raise awareness for the bills. And during the press conference, the Humane Society showed a video of children at a cockfight. The video disgusted me, and I thought, *This has to stop.*

I wanted to make real, tangible, and positive changes on behalf of animal welfare. The trip to Congress is another step toward fulfilling my promise to help more animals than I hurt.

Afterward, I did several big interviews with NPR (National Public Radio) and Fox News's Greta Van Susteren to let everyone know what we had been lobbying for. I'm just grateful that the Humane Society reached out to me, so that I could learn about animal welfare causes and be put in a position to help.

Between the 2010 and 2011 seasons, I had two different speaking engagements that were particularly meaningful to me.

First, I returned to prison—this time to talk to inmates with Coach Dungy, fulfilling a promise I had made to him earlier. Peter King covered it for *Sports Illustrated.*

It was such a pleasure to be in Coach Dungy's presence. I could listen to him talk all day. Every guy in that prison would have come out and spoken to him if they could. They were all in the windows to see him.

Speaking to those inmates was very hard for me to do. I was nervous—wondering what I was going to say, how I would deliver. Peter King was a little nervous too; I could see he was uncomfortable. I tried to help him relax, which in turn helped me. We got through it. He realized everyone was cool.

I decided to just speak from the heart. I spoke about some of my experiences and tried to encourage the guys. I just wanted to give them some insight. I spoke to two different groups, and I had a Q&A time with open dialogue. We laughed and joked and had a great time. I was glad to have done it and plan to do it again in the future.

The other opportunity was a bit more unique. I was chosen by the students from the Camelot schools—an alternative high school program in Philadelphia that serves at-risk youth—to be their commencement speaker. My speech to the approximately 450 graduates included these words:

> As you have chosen me, I want you to know that I've chosen you. I have chosen you to succeed. That's because I believe in you. You have proven your ability to overcome adversity, do the right thing, and finish school. You all are on my team. Take the lessons that you have learned, and apply them to your everyday life.

I was so blessed to announce that I would be funding $5,000

college scholarships for two of the students. It is a small way for me to provide hope and encouragement for others who are making the most of their second chance.

⌒

I've made it a priority in my life to dream again, and there's a Scripture passage that was shared with me recently that I find particularly encouraging. It's Isaiah 43:18–19:

> Forget the former things;
> do not dwell on the past.
> See, I am doing a new thing!
> Now it springs up; do you not perceive it?
> I am making a way in the wilderness
> and streams in the wasteland.

That's my life right there. It's like a promise from God as I look ahead and move forward. It exemplifies His heart for redemption.

All good quarterbacks must have good vision—an ability to see what defenses are doing ahead of time and discern what plays will work. They need to know just how far to throw a pass so it will land directly in a receiver's hands. Vision for life is important too, and that's something I have more of now than ever before.

My vision is to carry out God's plan and not do anything to interfere with what He has in store for me. I do that by being the best family man I can be, by not making irrational decisions, and by not surrounding myself with people who are bad influences.

On and off the field, it's all about staying the course. All the accolades are great, and all the things I've accomplished are good, but it's leaving a legacy that matters.

Obviously, inevitably, people are going to say, "Mike Vick was this; he did this; he did that." But remember me for what I accomplished after I matured—after the prison sentence.

I want to be remembered as a guy who never gave up, whether with my family, out on the football field, in a prison cell, or playing one-on-one basketball with someone in the neighborhood. To sum it all up, I would say one word: *resilient.* I stand firm in God, push through, and never give up—even in my darkest moments.

My job, my career, is simply what I do, not who I am. With this perspective—knowing my identity is in God and not in those things—I can move forward with confidence. In that confidence, I have set some goals for myself.

My goal in the NFL is simple: I want to win a Super Bowl.

What a moment it would be if one day I'm able to stand with my teammates and hold the Vince Lombardi Trophy that the NFL awards each year to its championship team. Every quarterback wants to lift up that trophy and say, "I led my team to a Super Bowl and won it." If I can accomplish that, it would be a storybook ending for me.

At the conclusion of my career, I want to take some time off and then eventually get into high school coaching to help as many kids as I can to get into college and teach them to dream big. I guess you could say I want to follow in Coach Tommy Reamon's footsteps, to pass along to others the many things he taught me.

I only want to coach high school. I won't coach college or the pros because those levels are just too time-consuming with recruiting and all the preparation that's necessary. I still want to have time with my family when I coach, and since I am already sacrificing family time, I don't want to do it again later in life.

Another thing I want to do, because I have the land, is to start a wildlife conservation center. I'd also like to have one or two animal shelters and open up two or three veterinary hospitals around the world. I think this would be a unique way for me to continue giving back. It can't fix what I've done, but it would provide a better future for animals.

Friends, fans, and fellow players have helped me to stay positive.

It meant a lot during the 2010 season to receive texts saying "Congratulations!" Teammates stood by me, and so did many players from other teams—guys like Peyton Manning. I am also thankful that support came from key people in my rehabilitation process—people who easily could have been very skeptical because of all that I did in the past. Words of support from the judge who sentenced me, the NFL commissioner who suspended me, and the Atlanta Falcons organization that I let down so severely were an incredible encouragement.

My comeback is far from over. I don't know if it will ever be fully complete, but I feel good that progress is being made. One of the ways I'm able to gauge how I'm doing is the feedback I get from the people who know me the best and have known me the longest—guys like Coach Reamon, Pastor Domeka Kelley, and James "Poo" Johnson from the Newport News Boys & Girls Club. Each of them has meant so much to me, both before and after my prison sentence. They encourage me almost daily, and I want to share with you some of their perspectives.

Coach Reamon says: "A tremendous maturity has happened in Michael. The football part doesn't surprise me at all, but his communication is also so solid for important things in his life and proving something, not just to himself but to others."

Pastor Kelley says he sees a noticeable difference in my countenance: "Michael has a smile that captivates the world. But now it's like he has a glow to go along with that smile. He has grown tremendously in his relationship with the Lord; he has found his purpose. He is a wonderful football player, but he knows he has a higher calling than that."

And here are a few words from Mr. Johnson: "One of the things I was so proud of was that Michael never got cold toward people. He has handled what has been said about him well. He manned up to it and didn't try to blame anyone else. He just stepped up and put the blame where it is supposed to be."

I greatly appreciate those words coming from men I admire so much. I know that it is God who has given me the grace to extend to others.

It's good to know that people from back home like Coach

Reamon, Pastor Kelley, and Mr. Johnson have my back. They follow and support virtually everything I do.

Mr. Johnson says he plays football vicariously through me and that he still views me as one of his kids in the Boys & Girls Club. "It's like every time you run the ball, I run the ball," he told me. "When you take a hit, I take a hit."

There are many areas I still need to improve in, both on and off the field. Mr. Johnson agrees with Coach Reid that, for my own safety, I need to become better at sliding at the end of a run rather than acting like a running back and subjecting myself to some rather crushing hits from defenders. Mr. Johnson even has an expert who he says can teach me: his longtime friend and base-ball Hall of Famer Willie Mays, who was an exceptional slider as well as a feared home-run hitter. Maybe one of the reasons I'm not a good slider is because, whether it's running with the football or giving a speech for the Humane Society or to a graduating class, I try to approach everything head-on.

Though there are times to approach life head-on, there are other times we need to let God do His thing.

⌐⌐

Philadelphia took a chance on me. Many people, like Andy Reid, Tony Dungy, and Roger Goodell, took a chance on me. Through it all—my rise, fall, and ongoing redemption—I had support. I had support from my family, friends, and fans. They didn't have to sup-port me, but they did. People didn't have to write me letters, but they did.

My story is not finished. I have more to do. I have something that I want to give back to everyone that supported me. Here it is: I am committed, focused, and determined to win a Super Bowl with the Philadelphia Eagles. This is my promise. It is my drive. I will work like a champion to get there. I want to do it for my family, friends, mentors, coaches, teammates, and fans. I want to do it for Philly.

~~

Not long before this book went to press, I went out to plant sunflower seeds with my son Mitez. I thought about what I would like to do with the sunflowers if they rose out of the ground: I told Mitez we'd take them and place them on my grandmother Caletha's grave. She's the one who taught me how to walk with confidence.

I wish she was still here to help me, because I know the eyes of the world are constantly on me, watching to see how—and if—I will grow. Watching to see if I will rise or fall. To the watching world, I'll say the same thing that I'd say to my grandmother if she were still with us: I've only just begun.

Postscript

Second chances are not any easier than the first; this is why we must learn from our failures and avoid repeating our mistakes. Based on my trials and successes, I have learned so much that is helping me now. I only wish I could have learned these things earlier.

I would like to share some principles that have helped me make the most of my second chance. I call them "seven keys to a better life." These principles are featured throughout this book, and it is my hope that they will be of some help to you too.

1. **Develop a relationship with God and put Him first in your life.**
2. **Honor and respect your family by making them a priority above other things and other relationships.**
3. **Build a positive and strong support network of peers by choosing your friends wisely.**
4. **Tell the truth in all situations. Lying will always backfire.**

5. Be mentored. We can learn so much from people wiser than ourselves. Then become a mentor, paying it forward to others.

6. Give hope and be an encouragement to others.

7. Pursue excellence in all you do through full commitment, sacrifice, and service.

Career Playing Record

(through the 2010 breakout season)

Player Profile

Full Name: Michael Dwayne Vick
Height: 6'0"
Weight: 215 pounds
Birthplace: Newport News, Va.
Birthdate: June 26, 1980
Parents: Brenda Vick and Michael Boddie
Siblings: Sisters - Christina & Courtney / Brother - Marcus
Wife: Kijafa Frink
Children: Son - Mitez / Daughters - Jada, London
High School: Ferguson and Warwick, Newport News, Va.
College: Virginia Tech, Blacksburg, Va.
First Team: Boys & Girls Club Spartans, Newport News, Va.
Greatest Influence: Grandmother - Caletha Vick
Favorite Childhood Athletes: Steve Young, Jerry Rice
Hobbies: Fishing, golf

Career Highlights

November 5, 1994	Second start as freshman for Ferguson vs. Gloucester, threw for 433 yards and 3 touchdowns
September 4, 1999	Debut for Virginia Tech vs. James Madison
January 4, 2000	Threw for 225 yards and rushed for 97 vs. Florida State in the 2000 Sugar Bowl
September 30, 2000	Rushed for 210 yards vs. Boston College
April 21, 2001	Drafted No. 1 overall by the Atlanta Falcons
September 9, 2001	Debut for Atlanta vs. San Francisco
September 23, 2001	Rushed for first career touchdown vs. Carolina
November 11, 2001	First NFL start and passing touchdown vs. Dallas
December 12, 2002	Threw for career-high 337 yards
January 4, 2003	First playoff victory vs. Green Bay (Wild Card) ending Green Bay's undefeated playoff record at Lambeau Field
February 2, 2003	First Pro Bowl
October 31, 2004	Became the first quarterback to throw for more than 250 yards and rush for more than 100 yards in the same game vs. Denver
December 24, 2005	Became the first quarterback in NFL history to rush for more than 1,000 yards in a single season with an 18-yard run vs. Carolina
September 27, 2009	Debut for Philadelphia vs. Kansas City
December 6, 2009	Scored first passing and rushing touchdowns in return to the NFL for Philadelphia vs. Atlanta
November 15, 2010	Threw for 333 yards and 4 touchdowns, and rushed for 80 yards and 2 touchdowns vs. Washington on *Monday Night Football* (game jersey enshrined in the Pro Football Hall of Fame)
January 30, 2011	First Pro Bowl start

Career Teams

Ferguson High School: 1994 - 1995
Warwick High School: 1996 - 1997
Virginia Tech: 1998 (Redshirted) - 2000
Atlanta Falcons: 2001 - 2006
Philadelphia Eagles: 2009 -

Career Statistical Profile

		Passing				Rushing	
	CMP	ATT	YDS	TD	INT	YDS	TD
HS: 94–97	234	523	4,846	44	28	958	16
College: 99–01	202	360	3,504	22	12	1,318	18
Pro: 01–06, 09–10	1,169	2,115	14,609	93	58	4,630	32

Season-by-Season Breakdown

			Passing				Rushing		
		G	C-A	YDS	TD	INT	No.	YDS	TD
Ferguson High	1994	3	19-46	487	3	3	17	-90	0
Ferguson High	1995	10	63-136	1,197	12	11	78	162	5
Warwick High	1996	10	59-123	1,494	19	6	98	267	3
Warwick High	1997	10	93-218	1,668	10	8	135	619	9
Virginia Tech	1999	11	105-181	2,065	13	5	131	682	9
Virginia Tech	2000	11	97-179	1,439	9	7	113	636	9
Atlanta Falcons	2001	8	50-113	785	2	3	31	289	1
Atlanta Falcons	2002	15	231-421	2,936	16	8	113	777	9
Atlanta Falcons	2003	5	50-100	585	4	3	40	255	1
Atlanta Falcons	2004	15	181-321	2,313	14	12	120	902	3
Atlanta Falcons	2005	15	214-387	2,412	15	13	102	597	6
Atlanta Falcons	2006	16	204-388	2,474	20	13	123	1,039	2
Philadelphia Eagles	2009	12	6-13	86	1	0	24	95	2
Philadelphia Eagles	2010	12	233-372	3,018	21	6	100	676	9

Game-by-Game Breakdown: High School

Ferguson High

			GS	Passing					Rushing		
				C–A	YDS	TD	INT	RTG	No.	YDS	TD
10.28.94	Phoebus	L 0-17	x	2-11	20	0	1	15.3	6	-34	0
11.05.94	Gloucester	W 41-14	x	13-15	433	3	0	395.1	4	-17	0
11.11.94	Kecoughton	L 0-14	x	4-20	34	0	2	14.3	17	-39	0
09.02.95	Lafayette	W 49-14	x	8-12	175	2	2	210.8	7	61	2
09.08.95	Menchville	W 10-6	x	4-10	80	0	2	67.2	6	40	1
09.15.95	Bethel	L 28-31	x	2-12	27	1	0	63.1	5	3	0
09.23.95	Tabb	W 13-6	x	4-14	105	1	1	100.9	3	-6	0
09.29.95	Denbigh	L 7-14	x	8-16	98	1	1	109.6	12	31	0
10.06.95	Warwick	W 24-0	x	6-10	84	0	1	110.6	9	-9	1
10.21.95	Hampton	L 14-27	x	11-17	154	1	1	148.5	12	17	1
10.27.95	Phoebus	L 17-20	x	5-12	129	1	1	142.8	8	-2	0
11.03.95	Gloucester	W 44-0	x	8-16	233	3	0	234.2	7	38	0
11.11.95	Kecoughton	L 20-34	x	7-17	112	2	2	111.8	9	-11	0

Warwick High

			GS	Passing					Rushing		
				C–A	YDS	TD	INT	RTG	No.	YDS	TD
08.31.96	Phoebus	L 7-23	x	6-20	92	1	2	65.1	10	-10	0
09.09.96	Heritage	W 57-0	x	4-7	107	2	0	279.8	4	60	0
09.14.96	Hampton	L 0-49	x	3-7	45	0	2	39.7	8	-39	0
09.27.96	Denbigh	W 20-0	x	3-12	60	1	0	94.5	12	98	1
10.05.96	Lafayette	W 26-0	x	10-17	174	2	1	71.9	11	64	1
10.11.96	Gloucester	W 20-7	x	6-12	243	1	0	247.6	2	22	0
10.18.96	Kecoughton	L 21-23	x	7-15	122	3	1	167.7	15	13	0
10.26.96	Menchville	W 33-3	x	7-13	176	2	0	218.3	12	64	0
11.02.96	Bethel	L 9-17	x	4-9	130	1	0	202.4	18	-61	0
11.08.96	Woodside	W 51-0	x	9-11	345	6	0	525.3	6	56	1
08.30.97	Phoebus	W 21-6	x	6-20	166	0	1	89.7	5	-16	0
09.09.97	Heritage	W 12-8	x	12-21	178	0	1	118.8	10	3	1
09.12.97	Hampton	L 16-34	x	17-39	295	1	1	110.5	13	39	1
09.19.97	Lakeland	L 18-32	x	9-32	114	0	3	39.3	14	133	2
09.26.97	Denbigh	W 19-6	x	4-11	93	1	1	119.2	19	124	1

				Passing					Rushing		
			GS	C-A	YDS	TD	INT	RTG	No.	YDS	TD
10.11.97	Gloucester	W 37-3	x	11-19	207	3	0	201.5	17	119	1
10.18.97	Kecoughton	L 7-14	x	6-14	108	0	1	93.4	25	14	1
10.24.97	Menchville	W 53-13	x	11-20	195	1	0	153.4	16	108	1
11.01.97	Bethel	W 17-0	x	5-13	171	2	0	199.7	9	8	0
11.08.97	Woodside	W 35-13	x	12-26	246	2	0	151.0	7	87	0

Note: Also had 73-yard and 35-yard punt returns for TDs that are not listed in his TD totals.

High School Career Summary

Record as a starter: 19-14

		Passing					Rushing		
	GS-GP	C-A	YDS	TD	INT	RTG	No.	YDS	TD
1994-95 Ferguson High	13-13	82-182	1,684	15	14	134.6	95	72	5
1996-97 Warwick High	20-20	152-341	3,162	29	14	142.3	233	886	12
HS TOTALS	**33-33**	**234-523**	**4,846**	**44**	**28**	**139.6**	**328**	**14**	**1**

Honors

1996 All-Peninsula District 1st team defense (DB)
1997 Preseason All-America by:
>   SuperPrep
>   PrepStar
1997 All-Peninsula District 1st team offense & defense (athlete & DB)
1997 All-America by:
>   SuperPrep
>   PrepStar
>   National Recruiting Advisor

Game-by-Game Breakdown: College

Virginia Tech

				Passing					Rushing		
			GS	C–A	YDS	TD	INT	RTG*	No.	YDS	TD
09.04.99	James Madison	W 47-0	x	4-6	110	0	0	220.7	4	54	3
09.23.99	Clemson	W 31-11	x	7-16	88	0	3	52.5	12	41	0
10.02.99	@ Virginia	W 31-7	x	7-9	222	1	0	321.6	10	40	0
10.09.99	@ Rutgers	W 58-20	x	11-12	248	4	0	375.3	8	68	1
10.16.99	Syracuse	W 62-0	x	8-16	135	1	0	141.5	12	6	0
10.30.99	@ Pittsburgh	W 30-17	x	10-17	170	1	0	162.2	11	70	1
11.06.99	@ West Virginia	W 22-20	x	14-30	255	0	0	118.1	9	50	0
11.13.99	Miami	W 43-10	x	11-23	151	0	0	102.9	14	46	0
11.20.99	@ Temple	W 62-7	x	7-10	171	2	2	239.6	12	134	2
11.26.99	Boston College	W 38-14	x	11-13	290	3	0	348.2	16	76	1
01.04.00	Sugar Bowl - BCS Championship										
	Florida State	L 29-46	x	15-29	225	1	0	128.3	23	97	1
09.02.00	Akron	W 52-23	x	7-11	186	2	1	247.5	8	102	2
09.07.00	@ East Carolina	W 45-28	x	9-15	106	1	0	141.4	6	13	0
09.16.00	Rutgers	W 49-0	x	10-18	120	1	0	129.9	11	104	1
09.30.00	@ Boston College	W 48-34	x	5-17	61	0	1	47.8	16	210	3
10.07.00	Temple	W 35-13	x	14-28	162	1	2	96.1	18	55	1
10.12.00	West Virginia	W 48-20	x	10-18	233	2	0	200.9	11	57	0
10.21.00	@ Syracuse	W 22-14	x	6-11	75	0	0	111.8	16	9	1
10.28.00	Pittsburgh	W 37-34	x	8-15	80	0	1	84.8	10	34	0
11.04.00	@ Miami	L 21-41		2-5	9	0	1	15.1	3	5	0
11.25.00	Virginia	W 42-21	x	16-23	202	1	0	157.7	5	28	0
01.01.01	Toyota Gator Bowl										
	Clemson	W 41-20	x	10-18	205	1	1	158.4	9	19	1

*NCAA Passer Rating

College Career Summary

Record as a starter: 19-0 (regular season) 1-1 (bowl games) 20-1 (overall)

	GS-GP	C-A	YDS	TD	INT	RTG*	No.	YDS	TD
			Passing					Rushing	
1999-00 Regular Season	19-20	177-313	3,074	20	14	145.8	201	1,202	16
2000-01 Bowl Games	2-2	25-47	430	2	1	139.8	32	116	2
VT TOTALS	**21-22**	**202-360**	**3,504**	**22**	**15**	**150.3**	**233**	**1,318**	**18**

*NCAA Passer Rating

Honors

1998 Paul Torgersen Award (VT top offensive newcomer)

1998 Iron Hokie Award (for performance in Spring strength and conditioning)

1999 All-Region East 1st team

1999 ECAC All-Star 1st team

1999 Virginia State Player of the Year (by state sports information directors)

1999 Freshman All-America 1st team
>   *Sporting News*
>   *Football News*

1999 All-BIG EAST 1st team

1999 BIG EAST Rookie of the Year

1999 BIG EAST Offensive Player of the Year

1999 All-America *Sporting News* 1st team

1999 All-America Associated Press 2nd team

1999 Archie Griffiin Award

1999 ESPY: National Player of the Year

1999 Virginia Tech Most Valuable Player

1999 3rd in Heisman Trophy voting (tied for highest finish ever by a freshman)

1999 Virginia Tech Most Valuable Player

2000 Super Iron Hokie Award (for performance in Spring strength testing)
>   Set positional record in back squat at 515 pounds
>   Ran second-fastest 40-yard dash in VT history: 4.25 seconds

2000 Preseason 1st team All-America

2000 All-BIG EAST 2nd team

Game-by-Game Breakdown:
Professional Career

Atlanta Falcons

			GS	C–A	YDS	TD	INT	RTG	No.	YDS	TD
				Passing					*Rushing*		
09.09.01	@ San Francisco	L 13-16		0-4	0	0	0	39.6	2	32	0
09.23.01	Carolina	W 24-16		2-2	27	0	0	118.8	3	23	1
10.07.01	Chicago	L 3-31		12-18	186	0	0	100.7	5	18	0
11.04.01	New England	L 10-24		2-9	56	0	0	53.0	2	50	0
11.11.01	Dallas	W 20-13	x	4-12	32	1	0	70.1	2	4	0
12.02.01	St. Louis	L 6-35		7-18	94	0	0	56.2	6	52	0
12.30.01	@ Miami	L 14-21		11-20	214	1	2	69.6	5	63	0
01.06.02	@ St. Louis	L 13-31	x	12-30	176	0	1	46.0	6	47	0

2001–02 Season: Elected to the Pro Bowl, but did not play in the game.

			GS	C–A	YDS	TD	INT	RTG	No.	YDS	TD
09.06.02	@ Green Bay	L 34-37	x	15-23	209	1	0	108.8	9	72	1
09.15.02	Chicago	L 13-14	x	17-28	166	1	0	89.3	10	56	0
09.22.02	Cincinnati	W 30-3	x	16-26	174	2	0	106.9	5	56	0
10.06.02	Tampa Bay	L 6-20	x	4-12	37	0	0	42.7	1	1	0
10.20.02	Carolina	W 30-0	x	16-22	178	0	0	96.4	6	91	1
10.27.02	@ New Orleans	W 37-35	x	16-24	195	0	0	91.5	10	91	2
11.03.02	Baltimore	W 20-17	x	12-24	136	0	1	50.0	7	-5	1
11.10.02	@ Pittsburgh	T 34-34	x	24-46	294	1	0	79.4	10	38	1
11.17.02	New Orleans	W 24-17	x	11-23	160	2	1	81.8	7	55	7
11.24.02	@ Carolina	W 41-0	x	19-24	272	2	0	141.7	5	20	0
12.01.02	@ Minnesota	W 30-24	x	11-28	173	1	1	57.6	10	173	2
12.08.02	@ Tampa Bay	L 10-34	x	12-25	125	1	1	59.6	6	9	0
12.15.02	Seattle	L 24-30	x	21-38	240	2	2	70.1	13	40	0
12.22.02	Detroit	W 36-15	x	20-38	337	2	1	89.5	8	42	0
12.29.02	@ Cleveland	L 16-24	x	17-40	240	1	1	60.4	6	38	0
01.04.03	NFC Wild Card										
	@ Green Bay	W 27-7	x	13-25	117	1	0	78.3	10	64	0
01.11.03	NFC Divisional Round										
	@ Philadelphia	L 6-20	x	22-38	274	0	2	58.4	6	30	0

		GS	C–A	YDS	TD	INT	RTG	No.	YDS	TD
			Passing					**Rushing**		
11.30.03	@ Houston	L 13-17		8-11	60	0	0	85.4	3	16	0
12.07.03	Carolina	W 20-14	x	16-33	179	0	1	52.5	14	141	1
12.14.03	@ Indianapolis	L 7-38	x	6-19	47	0	1	19.0	4	30	0
12.20.03	@ Tampa Bay	W 30-28	x	8-15	119	2	0	119.2	12	39	0
12.28.03	Jacksonville	W 21-14	x	12-22	180	2	1	93.0	7	29	0
09.12.04	@ San Francisco	W 21-19	x	13-22	163	1	1	78.4	6	10	0
09.19.04	St. Louis	W 34-17	x	14-19	179	1	0	120.3	12	109	0
09.26.04	Arizona	W 6-3	x	10-20	115	0	1	46.9	8	68	0
10.03.04	@ Carolina	W 27-10	x	10-18	148	0	0	82.6	7	35	0
10.10.04	Detroit	L 10-17	x	18-29	196	0	1	67.6	5	29	0
10.17.04	San Diego	W 21-20	x	12-21	218	2	1	104.9	9	35	1
10.24.04	@ Kansas City	L 10-56	x	7-21	119	0	2	13.9	6	62	0
10.31.04	@ Denver	W 41-28	x	18-24	252	2	0	13.1	12	115	0
11.14.04	Tampa Bay	W 24-14	x	8-16	147	1	1	76.8	9	73	0
11.21.04	@ NY Giants	W 14-10	x	12-20	115	2	0	109.4	15	104	0
11.28.04	New Orleans	W 24-21	x	16-29	212	2	1	87.1	10	69	1
12.05.04	@ Tampa Bay	L 0-27	x	13-27	115	0	2	29.1	8	81	0
12.12.04	Oakland	W 35-10	x	13-20	145	0	0	86.5	2	31	0
12.18.04	Carolina	W 34-31	x	11-28	154	2	2	51.8	8	68	1
01.02.05	@ Seattle	L 26-28	x	6-7	35	1	0	127.1	3	13	0
01.15.05	NFC Divisional Round										
	St. Louis	W 47-17	x	12-16	82	2	0	125.5	8	119	0
01.23.05	NFC Championship										
	@ Philadelphia	L 10-27	x	11-24	136	0	1	46.5	4	26	0
02.13.05	Pro Bowl										
	@ AFC	L 27-38		14-24	205	1	1	82.8	3	10	1
09.12.05	Philadelphia	W 14-10	x	12-23	156	0	1	55.7	11	68	1
09.18.05	@ Seattle	L 18-21	x	11-19	123	1	0	94.8	8	43	0
09.25.05	@ Buffalo	W 24-16	x	15-27	167	2	1	83.4	9	64	0

			GS	Passing C–A	YDS	TD	INT	RTG	Rushing No.	YDS	TD
10.02.05	Minnesota	W 30-10	x	6-8	49	1	0	129.7	4	58	0
10.16.05	@ New Orleans	W 34-31	x	11-23	112	1	1	58.6	8	51	0
10.24.05	NY Jets	W 27-14	x	11-26	116	0	3	16.3	9	18	2
11.06.05	@ Miami	W 17-10	x	22-31	228	1	0	102.6	8	38	0
11.13.05	Green Bay	L 25-33	x	20-30	209	2	0	108.9	7	20	1
11.20.05	Tampa Bay	L 27-30	x	21-38	306	2	0	99.2	4	17	0
11.24.05	@ Detroit	W 27-7	x	12-22	146	2	1	86.6	6	57	0
12.04.05	@ Carolina	L 6-24	x	17-35	171	0	2	39.1	4	27	0
12.12.05	New Orleans	W 36-17	x	12-23	231	1	1	83.8	6	38	2
12.18.05	@ Chicago	L 3-16	x	13-32	122	0	2	25.8	6	35	0
12.24.05	@ Tampa Bay	L 24-27	x	16-26	161	2	0	104.8	11	63	0
01.01.06	Carolina	L 11-44	x	15-24	115	0	1	56.8	1	0	0
02.12.06	Pro Bowl										
	AFC	L 17-23		4-12	69	1	1	46.9	2	17	0
09.10.06	@ Carolina	W 20-6	x	10-22	140	2	0	96.8	7	48	0
09.17.06	Tampa Bay	W 14-3	x	10-15	92	1	1	77.6	14	127	1
09.25.06	@ New Orleans	L 3-23	x	12-31	137	0	0	52.8	6	57	0
10.01.06	Arizona	W 32-10	x	13-22	153	0	1	61.4	11	101	0
10.15.06	NY Giants	L 14-27	x	14-27	154	0	1	53.6	8	68	1
10.22.06	Pittsburgh	W 41-38	x	18-30	232	4	2	96.1	5	40	0
10.29.06	@ Cincinnati	W 29-27	x	19-27	291	3	0	142.7	9	55	0
11.05.06	@ Detroit	L 14-30	x	17-32	163	1	2	52.0	10	80	0
11.12.06	Cleveland	L 13-17	x	16-40	197	1	2	52.0	7	74	0
11.19.06	@ Baltimore	L 20-24	x	11-21	127	1	0	86.8	6	54	0
11.26.06	New Orleans	L 13-31	x	9-24	84	0	0	47.9	12	166	0
12.03.06	@ Washington	W 24-14	x	8-16	122	2	0	115.1	10	59	0
12.10.06	@ Tampa Bay	W 17-6	x	14-23	155	0	1	62.8	3	5	0
12.16.06	Dallas	L 28-38	x	16-24	237	4	1	121.0	8	56	0
12.24.06	Carolina	L 3-10	x	9-20	109	0	2	22.7	4	32	0
12.31.06	@ Philadelphia	L 17-24	x	8-14	81	1	0	97.6	3	17	0

Philadelphia Eagles

			GS	C–A	YDS	TD	INT	RTG	No.	YDS	TD
				Passing					**Rushing**		
09.27.09	Kansas City	W 34-14		0-2	0	0	0	39.6	1	7	0
10.11.09	Tampa Bay	W 33-14		1-3	1	0	0	42.4	4	10	0
10.18.09	@ Oakland	L 9-13		0-0	0	0	0	0.0	1	-4	0
10.26.09	@ Washington	W 27-17		1-1	5	0	0	87.5	3	9	0
11.01.09	NY Giants	W 40-17		0-0	0	0	0	0.0	2	3	0
11.08.99	Dallas	L 13-20		0-0	0	0	0	0.0	1	2	0
11.15.09	@ San Diego	L 23-31		0-1	0	0	0	39.6	0	0	0
11.22.09	@ Chicago	W 24-20		1-1	0	0	0	79.2	1	34	0
11.29.09	Washington	W 27-24		0-1	0	0	0	39.6	2	4	0
12.06.09	@ Atlanta	W 34-7		2-2	48	1	0	158.3	4	17	1
12.13.09	@ NY Giants	W 45-38		1-2	32	0	0	95.8	3	11	1
12.20.09	San Francisco	W 27-13	x	0-0	0	0	0	0.0	2	2	0
01.09.10	NFC Wild Card										
	@ Dallas	L 14-34		1-2	76	1	0	135.4	1	0	0
09.12.10	Green Bay	L 20-27		16-24	175	1	0	101.9	11	103	0
09.19.10	@ Detroit	W 35-32	x	21-34	284	2	0	108.0	8	37	2
09.29.10	@ Jacksonville	W 28-3	x	17-31	291	3	0	119.2	4	30	1
10.03.10	Washington	L 12-17	x	5-7	49	0	0	90.8	3	17	0
11.07.10	Indianapolis	W 26-24	x	17-29	218	1	0	93.7	10	74	0
11.15.10	@ Washington	W 59-28	x	20-28	333	4	0	150.7	8	80	2
11.21.10	NY Giants	W 27-17	x	24-38	258	0	0	83.0	11	34	2
11.28.10	@ Chicago	L 26-31	x	29-44	333	2	1	94.2	9	44	0
12.02.10	Houston	W 34-24	x	22-33	302	2	1	103.3	10	48	1
12.12.10	@ Dallas	W 30-27	x	16-26	270	2	2	90.2	8	16	1
12.19.10	@ NY Giants	W 38-31	x	21-35	242	3	1	97.6	10	130	1
12.28.10	Minnesota	L 14-24	x	25-43	263	1	1	74.1	8	63	1
01.09.11	NFC Wild Card										
	Green Bay	L 16-21	x	20-36	292	1	1	79.9	8	32	1
01.30.11	Pro Bowl										
	AFC	L 41-55	x	5-10	59	0	0	68.3	0	0	0

Professional Career Summary

Record as a starter:

46-30-1 (regular season) 2-3 (playoffs) 0-1 (Pro Bowls) 48-34-1 (overall)

			Passing					Rushing	
	GS-GP	C-A	YDS	TD	INT	RTG	No.	YDS	TD
2000-06 Atlanta Falcons	65-74	930-1,730	11,505	71	52	75.7	529	3,859	21
2009-10 Philadelphia Eagles	12-24	239-375	3,104	22	6	102.6	124	771	11
Playoffs	5-6	79-141	977	5	4	77.6	37	271	1
Pro Bowls	1-3	23-46	333	2	2	70.3	5	27	1
PROFESSIONAL TOTALS	**83-107**	**1,271-2,309**	**15,919**	**100**	**64**	**79.6**	**695**	**4,928**	**34**

Honors

4-time Pro Bowl selection: 2002, 2004, 2005, 2010

2003 ESPY: Best NFL Player

2009 Ed Block Courage Award (Philadelphia Eagles)

2010 Comeback Player of the Year

        Associated Press

        Sporting News

        Pro Football Weekly

2010 Bert Bell NFL Player of the Year (Maxwell Football Club)

2010 NFC Offensive Player of the Year (Kansas City 101 Awards)

2011 Subway Sportsman of the Year (BET Awards)

NFL Records

- First in NFL history to throw for 3,000+ yards and 20+ touchdowns, rush for 500+ yards and 7+ touchdowns in a season.

- Most 100-yard rushing games by a QB: 11

- Most rushing yards by a QB in a season: 1,039 (2006)

- Highest yards-per-carry average in a season, minimum 100 attempts: 8.45 (2006)

- Most rushing yards in a game by a QB: 173
- Most rushing yards in a playoff game by a QB: 119
- Highest two-game rushing total by a QB: 225
- Most rushing yards by a QB in first two seasons: 1,066

Career Game: MONDAY NIGHT VICK-TORY

Monday, November 15, 2010, 8:30 p.m.
Philadelphia Eagles (5-2) at Washington Redskins (4-4)

FedEx Field - 52°, Raining
Head Official: Clete Blakeman
Attendance - 84,912

Box Score

Game Summary

	1	2	3	4	F
PHIL	28	17	14	0	59
WAS	0	14	7	7	28

Team Stats

	Eagles	Redskins
First downs	28	15
Rushes-Yards	38-260	18-105
Passing Yards	332	270
Sacked-Yards Lost	1-1	2-25
Return Yardage	149	175
Passing	20-28-0	17-31-3
Punts-Average	4-39.8	6-50.0
Fumbles-Lost	2-0	1-0
Penalties-Yards	6-35	6-41
Field Goals	1-1	0-0
Red Zone Efficiency	4-4-100%	3-3-100%
Goal To Go Efficiency	4-4-100%	3-3-100%
Time of Possession	38:11	21:49

Scoring Summary

1st Quarter - 14:42	
TD	Redskins 0 - Eagles 7
DeSean Jackson 88 yd. pass from Michael Vick (David Akers kick)	
1st Quarter - 10:17	
TD	Redskins 0 - Eagles 14
Michael Vick 7 yd. run (David Akers kick)	
1st Quarter - 5:02	
TD	Redskins 0 - Eagles 21
LeSean McCoy 11 yd. pass from Michael Vick (David Akers kick)	
1st Quarter - 1:55	
TD	Redskins 0 - Eagles 28
Jerome Harrison 50 yd. run (David Akers kick)	
2nd Quarter - 14:51	
TD	Redskins 0 - Eagles 35
Jeremy Maclin 48 yd. pass from Michael Vick (David Akers kick)	
2nd Quarter - 14:15	
TD	Redskins 7 - Eagles 35
Darrel Young 3 yd. pass from Donovan McNabb (Graham Gano kick)	
2nd Quarter - 9:39	
TD	Redskins 14 - Eagles 35
Keiland Williams 6 yd. pass from Donovan McNabb (Graham Gano kick)	
2nd Quarter - 3:34	
TD	Redskins 14 - Eagles 42
Michael Vick 6 yd. run (David Akers kick)	

2nd Quarter - 0:25	
FG	Redskins 14 - Eagles 45
David Akers 48 yd. field goal	
3rd Quarter - 11:27	
TD	Redskins 21 - Eagles 45
Keiland Williams 4 yd. run (Graham Gano kick)	
3rd Quarter - 6:15	
TD	Redskins 21 - Eagles 52
Jason Avant 3 yd. pass from Michael Vick (David Akers kick)	
3rd Quarter - 5:19	
TD	Redskins 21 - Eagles 59
Dimitri Patterson 40 yd. interception return (David Akers kick)	
4th Quarter - 11:16	
TD	Redskins 28 - Eagles 59
Keiland Williams 32 yd. run (Graham Gano kick)	

Player Stats - Philadelphia Eagles

Passing	CP/ATT	YDS	TD	INT	LG
Michael Vick	20/28	333	4	0	88

Rushing	ATT	YDS	TD	LG
Jerome Harrison	11	109	1	50
Michael Vick	8	80	2	21
LeSean McCoy	11	43	0	9
Eldra Buckley	5	13	0	9
Jeremy Maclin	1	11	0	11
DeSean Jackson	1	5	0	5
Kevin Kolb	1	-1	0	-1

Receiving	TAR	REC	YDS	TD	LG
DeSean Jackson	3	2	98	1	88
Jeremy Maclin	6	4	79	1	48
Jason Avant	5	5	76	1	27
LeSean McCoy	6	5	51	1	27
Jerome Harrison	1	1	15	0	15
Brent Celek	4	2	8	0	7
Owen Schmitt	2	1	6	0	6
Riley Cooper	1	0	0	0	0

Kicking	FG	LG	XP	PTS
David Akers	1/1	48	8/8	11

Punting	NO	AVG	I20	LG
Sav Rocca	4	38.3	4	53

Kickoff Returns	NO	AVG	TD	LG
Jorrick Calvin	4	16	0	24

Punt Returns	NO	AVG	TD	LG
Jorrick Calvin	3	8	0	14
DeSean Jackson	1	12	0	12

Interceptions	NO	YDS	TD
Dimitri Patterson	2	40	1
Kurt Coleman	1	7	0

Sacks	NO	YDS
Trevor Laws	1	13
Juqua Parker	1	12

Tackles	TK	AST
Dimitri Patterson	5	0
Kurt Coleman	4	1
Stewart Bradley	3	5
Moise Fokou	2	0
Quintin Mikell	2	2
Brodrick Bunkley	1	0
Akeem Jordan	1	0

Asante Samuel	1	0
Colt Anderson	1	0
Trevor Laws	1	0
Darryl Tapp	1	0
Juqua Parker	1	0
Jamar Chaney	1	1
Mike Patterson	1	2
Trent Cole	1	3
Antonio Dixon	0	1
Keenan Clayton	0	1
Ernie Sims	0	1

Fumbles	NO	LOST
DeSean Jackson	1	0
Jorrick Calvin	1	0

Player Stats - Washington Redskins

Passing	CP/ATT	YDS	TD	INT	LG
Donovan McNabb	17/31	295	2	3	76

Rushing	ATT	YDS	TD	LG
Keiland Williams	16	89	2	32
Darrel Young	1	16	0	16
Donovan McNabb	1	0	0	0

Receiving	TAR	REC	YDS	TD	LG
Anthony Armstrong	5	3	83	0	76
Fred Davis	1	1	71	0	71
Keiland Williams	7	4	50	1	26
Santana Moss	5	3	28	0	13
Mike Sellers	1	1	28	0	28
Chris Cooley	7	3	23	0	11
Roydell Williams	2	1	9	0	9
Darrel Young	1	1	3	1	3
Joey Galloway	2	0	0	0	0

Kicking	FG	LG	XP	PTS
Graham Gano	0/0	0	4/4	4

Punting	NO	AVG	I20	LG
Hunter Smith	6	44.0	1	56

Kickoff Returns	NO	AVG	TD	LG
Brandon Banks	6	26	0	38
Mike Sellers	1	11	0	11

Punt Returns	NO	AVG	TD	LG
Brandon Banks	1	6	0	6

Interceptions	NO	YDS	TD
No interceptions			

Sacks	NO	YDS
Andre Carter	0.5	0.5
Brian Orakpo	0.5	0.5

Tackles	TK	AST
London Fletcher	9	4
LaRon Landry	6	3
DeAngelo Hall	5	3
André Carter	4	3
Kedric Golston	3	1
Rocky McIntosh	3	1
Carlos Rogers	3	2
Brian Orakpo	3	5
Phillip Buchanon	2	0
Kareem Moore	2	4
Adam Carriker	1	0
Phillip Daniels	1	0
Reed Doughty	1	0
Albert Haynesworth	1	0
Ma'ake Kemoeatu	1	2
Lorenzo Alexander	1	2

Fumbles	NO	LOST
Donovan McNabb	1	0

List of Illustrations

Michael Vick is the quarterback for the Philadelphia Eagles of the National Football League. The 2010 season was the most prolific of his career, earning him a start in the Pro Bowl and cementing his comeback in football. Prior to spending the past three seasons with the Philadelphia Eagles, Michael played for the Atlanta Falcons (2001–2006), the team that originally chose him with the first overall pick in the 2001 NFL draft.

Brett Honeycutt is the managing editor of *Sports Spectrum* magazine, a national faith-based sports publication that has been around for more than twenty-eight years. Prior to taking his current position, he worked for the *Charlotte Observer* for sixteen years (six years as a freelance writer and ten years on staff). Brett is a graduate of Liberty University in Lynchburg, Virginia, and is from Charlotte, North Carolina.

Stephen Copeland is the editor of *Sports Spectrum*'s digital magazine and a columnist at *Sports Spectrum* magazine, a national faith-based sports publication. He recently coauthored *The Jersey Effect* with former Indianapolis Colts punter Hunter Smith. Stephen graduated from Grace College in Winona Lake, Indiana, and is from Plainfield, Indiana.

WORTHY
PUBLISHING

IF YOU LIKED THIS BOOK . . .

- Tell your friends by going to: http://finallyfreebook.com and clicking "LIKE"

- Share the video book trailer by posting it on your Facebook page

- Log on to our Facebook page, click "LIKE" and post a comment regarding what you enjoyed about the book

- Tweet "I recommend reading #FinallyFreeBook by @MikeVick"

- Hashtag: #FinallyFreeBook

- Subscribe to our newsletter by going to http://worthy publishing.com/about/subscribe.php

WORTHY PUBLISHING
FACEBOOK PAGE

WORTHY PUBLISHING
WEBSITE